ENDORSEMENTS

"In a world where so many vainly attempt to deny the truth—or deny that truth can be known at all—Dr. Steven Lawson reminds us, 'Thus says the Lord.' This is vintage Lawson—the raising of a prophetic voice keenly aware of the vagaries of the age and resolute in pointing us to the life-giving truth of God's Word and the gospel."

—Dr. Stephen J. Nichols
President, Reformation Bible College
Sanford, Fla.

"We live in the most anti-intellectual and anti-theological era in the history of the church, and that's because the church has too often taken its marching orders from the culture. When the culture denies the existence of objective truth and the church follows the culture, then of course the church is going to turn away from loving God with her mind. We need men in the church who are committed to the objective truth of the gospel, and that is why I'm grateful that God has raised up Steve Lawson for such a time as this. His passionate commitment to the truth and the difference it makes in the Christian life shines through this work. I believe *The Moment of Truth* will serve Christians well as they seek to be faithful to the objective truth of God's Word."

—Dr. R.C. Sproul
Founder, Ligonier Ministries
Orlando, Fla.

THE MOMENT
OF TRUTH

STEVEN J. LAWSON

Ⅸ *Reformation Trust*   A DIVISION OF LIGONIER MINISTRIES, ORLANDO, FL

The Moment of Truth
© 2018 by Steven J. Lawson

Published by Reformation Trust Publishing
A division of Ligonier Ministries
421 Ligonier Court, Sanford, FL 32771
Ligonier.org   ReformationTrust.com

Printed in York, Pennsylvania
Maple Press
February 2018
First edition

ISBN 978-1-56769-855-8 (Hardcover)
ISBN 978-1-56769-918-0 (ePub)
ISBN 978-1-56769-919-7 (Kindle)

Cover design: Vanessa Wingo
Interior design and typeset: Nord Compo

Unless otherwise noted, Scripture quotations are from the ESV® Bible (The Holy Bible, English Standard Version®), copyright © 2001 by Crossway, a publishing ministry of Good News Publishers. Used by permission. All rights reserved.

Scripture quotations marked NASB are taken from the New American Standard Bible® (NASB), Copyright © 1960, 1962, 1963, 1968, 1971, 1972, 1973, 1975, 1977, 1995 by The Lockman Foundation. Used by permission. www.Lockman.org

Library of Congress Cataloging-in-Publication Data

Names: Lawson, Steven J., author.
Title: The moment of truth / Steven J. Lawson.
Description: Orlando, FL : Reformation Trust Publishing, 2018. | Includes
   bibliographical references and index.
Identifiers: LCCN 2017036643 (print) | LCCN 2017045200 (ebook) | ISBN
   9781567699180 (ePub) | ISBN 9781567699197 (Kindle) | ISBN
9781567698558
Subjects: LCSH: Truth—Religious aspects—Christianity.
Classification: LCC BT50 (ebook) | LCC BT50 .L39 2018 (print) | DDC 230–dc23
LC record available at https://lccn.loc.gov/2017036643

To Bill Dunlap

A long-standing, faithful friend who has encouraged
my ministry for almost forty years and
who helped me launch OnePassion Ministries

CONTENTS

Part 1

THE REALITY
OF TRUTH

1

WHAT IS TRUTH?

The Reality of Truth in a Fallen World

"Does absolute truth exist?"

The question is often asked by many today.

We live in a generation that denies any such notion of truth. The only absolute seems to be there are no absolutes, and the only truth that there is no truth. These statements are not theoretical, but, sadly, represent the mind-set of our postmodern world. We commonly hear people today say, "You have your truth, and I have my truth." In the contemporary marketplace of ideas, personal opinions and crass pragmatism are the currency that buys and sells.

The blatant rejection of absolute truth is nothing new but can be traced many centuries back. We hear its denial echo through the corridors of time, all the way back to the life and ministry of our Lord Jesus Christ. The night before His crucifixion, Jesus stood trial before Pontius Pilate and engaged in a one-on-one conversation in which Pilate's own denunciation of truth was clearly revealed. He had heard Jesus speak of His kingdom and proclaim that He was a king. Upon Jesus' assertion that everyone who was of the truth would hear His voice, Pilate skeptically retorted, "What is truth?" (John 18:38).

This is the age-old question that was voiced by Pilate as he stood face-to-face before the One who is Truth incarnate. This was not an honest question raised by one searching to know the truth. Rather, it was a defiant denial that there is any such thing as truth. Pilate's statement was spoken with utter contempt—a dismissive chide dripping with sarcasm. This rebuttal was intended to belittle the speculation of any truth claim in the world. Spoken with a harsh tone of derision, this pushback was a barbed jab by Pilate at the Lord Jesus Christ. It was intended to denigrate the idea that anyone—much less Jesus—could claim to know and speak the truth. Pilate categorically rejected the very idea of an exclusive truth claim.

This fundamental question "What is truth?" has reverberated down through the centuries and has continued to grow louder into this present hour. With increasing volume, we hear the repeated mantra, "What is truth?" The spirit of Pilate lives stronger today than ever before. This unbelief is alive and well on college campuses. It reigns in the halls of government. It legislates our public morality and reigns in our media. It teaches in many seminaries and stands in countless pulpits. We live in a culture that is relentlessly defiant of any thought of exclusive truth. In fact, our society not only questions the reality of truth, but it has become vehemently anti-truth. We are tolerant of anyone and anything except one who claims to know absolute truth.

The elements of this conversation between Jesus and Pilate represent a microcosm of the battle that rages over the existence of God's truth in our world today. This confrontation begins with Pilate's emphatic rejection of truth, progresses to Jesus' affirmation of the reality of truth, and culminates with Jesus' assertion of the reign of truth in the lives of believers. As we view this dialogue between Jesus and Pilate through these three lenses, we are able to find penetrating insight and broader applications for our lives today. This threefold perspective will prepare us to effectively uphold the truth in our day.

The Rejection of Truth

In uttering the words "What is truth?" Pilate issued an unequivocal rejection of the existence of ultimate truth. This disregard of the truth is as grave a sin as it is ancient. We see it from the beginning of creation, when Satan the serpent first slithered onto the pages of human history and launched his original temptation to reject the truth. This was his attempt to create a world in which the rejection of truth would run rampant. The rejection of the truth is where sin began, and it continues to this day.

With this in mind, Paul writes, "For the wrath of God is revealed from heaven against all ungodliness and unrighteousness of men, who by their unrighteousness suppress the truth" (Rom. 1:18). Whenever the truth of God is suppressed, it always leads to believing a lie. "Because they exchanged the truth about

God for a lie, and worshiped and served the creature rather than the Creator" (Rom. 1:25). This rejection of the truth is the demise of any individual life and the destruction of any corporate society. The downward spiral always begins with the rejection of the truth.

Continually and increasingly, our postmodern society has exchanged the truth of God for a lie. This egregious substitution has had serious consequences for people's lives and for our pluralistic culture. Years ago, Allan Bloom, a noted college professor, wrote a book titled *The Closing of the American Mind.* As he instructed the brightest students of his day, he wrote that 95 percent of all entering college students were avowed relativists who rejected any notion of definitive truth. By the time they graduated, 97 percent of the students rejected any claim to exclusive truth whatsoever. No culture can long survive such a denial. This all-out refusal to recognize the truth is hitting our society like a tsunami, and its breakers have submerged the majority of modern minds.

One astute philosopher has said that we are raising a generation of "moral stutterers." Others call it "moral illiteracy." Yet another observer says, "There is a hole in our moral ozone." This has produced an imploding world in which abortion, homosexuality, euthanasia, pornography, transgender identity, and all manner of lewd behavior are practiced and approved of. This abandonment of moral values can be traced back to the rejection of the truth. When absolute truth departs, everything is up for grabs. Tragically, modern man now has his feet firmly planted in midair.

The supreme sin today, it seems, is not the committing of moral wickedness. Rather, it is making an exclusive claim of absolute truth. The unpardonable sin in this generation is to affirm moral absolutes. The abomination of the hour is to assert that the Bible is the authoritative standard of truth and to maintain that all that is contrary to the truth is a lie. Such is an anathema in the truth-rejecting world of the twenty-first century.

Many Claims for Truth

This defection from the standard of absolute truth has resulted in multiple truth claims. Humanism says man is the truth. Pragmatism says whatever works is the truth. Pluralism says everyone has a piece of the truth. Relativism says each situation determines the truth. Mysticism says intuition is the truth. Skepticism says no one can know the truth. Heathenism says whatever feels good is the truth. Existentialism says self-determination is the truth. Secularism says this present world is the truth. Positivism says whatever man confesses is the truth. This is the world in which we live—a world that rejects the claim of any absolute truth that is the standard for everyone.

This universal rejection of absolute truth is what we face as we live in this world. We are surrounded by the taunts of this world that question, "What is truth?" Maybe this is what you face in your work environment. Perhaps this is what confronts you at your family reunions. There is a strong probability that this is what confronts you on your college campus. And this is exactly what Jesus faced when He stood before Pilate. In this sense, you are in good company. So, let us investigate how the Lord responded in His confrontation.

The Reality of Truth

As Jesus stood trial that day, He affirmed that there is truth. Moreover, Jesus maintained that there is *the* truth. He informed Pilate that His reason for coming into the world was to teach and affirm the truth. By this statement, Jesus claimed to have an exclusive monopoly on *the* truth. In fact, Jesus asserted that He Himself is the truth. The Apostle Paul affirmed this when he wrote, "truth is in Jesus" (Eph. 4:21). In other words, all truth is in Jesus Christ, who is the very incarnation and embodiment of truth.

How can we define truth? The word *truth* (Greek *alētheia*) means "a reality that is firm, solid, binding." It represents that which has certainty and that on which one can rely. In a word, truth is reality. Truth is how anything really is. Truth is not how things may appear to be. Nor is it how we want things to be. Neither is it what opinion polls say something is. To the contrary, truth is the way things really are. What identifies its chief characteristics? There are eight reference points that help us distinguish what Frances Schaeffer called "true truth" from pretenders to the truth.

What follows are eight distinguishing marks of what constitutes the truth. Each is a critical link on a chain that provides us with a comprehensive view of the truth.

Truth Comes from God

First, truth is *divine*. That is to say, all truth originates with God. Truth does not come from man. It is not derived from this world. Nor does it arise from the collected thoughts of society and culture. It is not determined by the majority opinion. To the contrary, truth comes down from God above. God the Father is "the God of truth" (Ps. 31:5, NASB), God the Son is "the truth" (John 14:6), God the Holy Spirit is "the Spirit of truth" (John 14:17; 15:26; 16:13). All three persons of the Godhead are truth. In this sense, truth is Trinitarian. Each person of the Trinity is the standard of all truth, and They speak only the truth. Their words are true, and Their judgments are governed by truth. All three persons—Father, Son, and Holy Spirit—think, speak, and act the truth.

So, what is truth? It is the self-revelation of God's own being—the self-disclosure of the nature, mind, and will of God. The author of all truth is God. He is the sole determiner of truth, the supreme governor of truth, and the highest arbitrator of truth. As the ultimate standard of truth, God Himself measures all things. All that is in agreement with what God is, says, and does is truth. In this sense, God is the final judge of all truth. Therefore, sin is whatever God says it is. Heaven and hell are exactly what God says they are. Salvation is what God says it is. Morality and the family are what God says they are. The Scripture says, "Let God be true though every one were a liar" (Rom. 3:4).

Truth is an out-of-this-world entity. It comes down from another realm. It comes from the character and mind of God

Himself. Therefore, if you are to know the truth, you must not look to yourself. You must not poll the world to find it. You must look to God and His Word as the only source of ultimate truth.

Truth Reigns Supremely

Second, truth is *absolute*. This is to say, truth reigns as the highest authority in determining all matters. Everything yields to the truth. Truth has the first word and the final say in every matter. In this sense, truth is sovereign. It is exclusive, not inclusive. Truth draws a sharp line between what is and what is not truth. Thus, truth is discriminating. Truth makes fine distinctions between what is right and wrong. It is never both/and but is always either/or. Truth is never relative, arbitrary, or conditional. It is always conclusive and unconditional. Everything outside of it is false by definition, while everything inside the truth is true.

By contrast, Satan is a liar and the Father of Lies. His servants speak his native tongue of falsehoods. He is "the god of this age" (2 Cor. 4:4), "the ruler of this world" (John 12:31), and "the prince of the power of the air" (Eph. 2:2). This evil world system is filled with his lies. Ultimately, there are only two fathers in the world, with two families. The first family is made up of those who belong to God, and they alone hear the truth. The second family has the devil for their father, and they reject God's truth, just as Pilate did.

Truth Is a Fact

Third, truth is *objective*. That is to say, truth is propositional. It is stated in clearly defined words that have a precise meaning. Truth speaks with specific words that have a definite meaning. It is concrete, black and white, and narrowly defined. It never blurs the lines of distinction. It never speaks in ambiguous terms. Truth is never vague or fuzzy. It is razor sharp; it focuses like a laser beam. It is explicit, exact, and crystal clear in its meaning. Truth is factual, rational, and tangible. It is based not upon subjective feelings but upon objective facts.

Specifically, truth is contained in the written Word of God. It is expressed in actual words that can be studied and interpreted. And it is true regardless of how anyone feels about it. It is always true, whether it speaks subjectively to any given individual or not. Truth is truth either way. It does not have to be believed in order to be truth. When God speaks, He speaks what is truth. God has not stuttered or mumbled when He has spoken His truth.

All Truth Stands Together

Fourth, truth is *singular*. As Jesus represented the truth before Pilate, He spoke of *the* truth as one entity. The definite article *the* distinguishes it from merely being *a* truth. When Jesus asserted *the* truth, He was stressing that all truth is one system of revealed reality. Every piece of truth perfectly fits together into one body of divinity. Truth never contradicts itself. Truth is never at odds with itself. Truth never speaks out of both sides of its mouth.

Truth is never canceled out by another truth claim. What God says to one person is what He says to everyone else. Truth is never true for one person, but not true for someone else. Truth is always truth for every individual.

Frances Schaeffer wrote years ago, "Christianity is not just a lot of bits and pieces—there is a beginning and an end, a whole system of truth, and this system is the only system that will stand up to all the questions that are presented to us as we face the reality of existence."[1] That is, the Bible always speaks with one voice, as it is always presenting one self-consistent worldview. Whenever the truth speaks, it makes the same diagnosis of the problem of the human condition. It sets forth one plan of salvation for fallen humanity. It presents one history of redemption for the ages. It offers one Savior of sinners to the world. It offers one remedy of eternal life. It presents one self-consistent worldview as the lens through which we see everything.

All of the sixty-six books of the Bible hang together. Each portion of Scripture speaks in perfect harmony with every other part of it. Like a finely woven tapestry, the threads of truth are perfectly interwoven throughout all the Scripture. If you pull a thread in Genesis, the Bible crinkles in Revelation. There is the golden cord of God's sovereign rule over the world that is woven throughout the whole Bible. There is also the red cord of redemption that runs all the way through Scripture. Throughout

1. Francis A. Schaeffer, *The God Who Is There,* in *The Complete Works of Francis Schaeffer: A Christian Worldview,* 5 vols. (Wheaton, Ill.: Crossway, 1982), 1:178.

the pages of the Bible, there is one consistent presentation of the truth. This reality affirms that truth is singular, never pluralistic, never in disharmony with itself. All truth is in perfect accord with every other truth. Therefore, what a person believes about one truth will indicate what he believes about a host of other truths because it is all fused together.

Truth Never Changes

Fifth, truth is likewise *immutable*. God does not change, and neither does His truth. What was true in the garden of Eden is true throughout the whole of the Old Testament. It remained true in the time of Christ and throughout the expansion of the church, and it remains true to this present hour. The truth never ceases to be. It remains true from one generation to the next, from one age to the next age. What is truth today never becomes untrue tomorrow. Right is always right, and wrong is always wrong. Society tries to redefine morality, and culture tries to reclassify right and wrong, but truth never changes its mind. It is unalterably fixed, permanently established, and unwaveringly constant. Truth rises above time and transcends the centuries. Truth is timeless, forever anchored and eternal.

The psalmist declared, "Forever, O LORD, your word is firmly fixed in the heavens" (Ps. 119:89). Isaiah 40:8 says, "The grass withers, the flowers fades, but the word of our God will stand forever." Therefore, truth is always up to date, it is always contemporary, and it always addresses the issues of the day. Truth is never outdated, never archaic. It has a long shelf life, with no expiration date. Nothing new can ever replace it, and it never becomes obsolete.

Years ago, I was a student in law school and stayed up long nights in order to analyze and scrutinize the law. One thing I discovered was that the law I examined at the beginning of the semester had often changed by the time I came to the final exam. It was frustrating to realize that I had invested so much time in studying a changing law. At that same time, I was beginning to study and preach God's Word. One day, it struck me that part of my attraction to God's Word is that it never changes. The investment of my time in studying the Scripture abides with me permanently and never needs to be updated or changed. I will never wake up one day and find that something that was once true will become untrue. Neither will there be any new truth.

Truth Makes Demands

Sixth, truth is *authoritative*. What God has spoken in His written Word is supremely authoritative. Nothing can overrule the truth. Truth is like an enthroned monarch who rules over our lives sovereignly. When the truth speaks, it drowns out every other voice. No philosophy, religion, or mere human opinion can cancel out the truth. Truth has the right to make assertive demands upon our lives. Truth necessitates something from us. When the Bible speaks, God Himself speaks and summons us by His truth.

Truth is never intended to be merely interesting. It is never meant to simply stimulate our curiosity. Truth is never meant to be an intellectual pursuit in itself. We can never tip our hat politely at truth and walk on our own way. Truth is never a suggestion to consider, never an option to weigh. Truth places a responsibility upon us to act. Truth has the right to make assertive demands upon our lives because it speaks with the sovereignty of God. It possesses the right to rule our lives and must be obeyed. Truth calls for our response.

Truth Cuts Deeply

Seventh, truth is *powerful*. It cuts us deeply, both convicting and challenging us. Hebrews 4:12 states, "For the word of God is living and active, sharper than any two-edged sword, piercing to the division of soul and of spirit, of joints and of marrow, and discerning the thoughts and intentions of the heart." That is to say, the truth of the Word of God cuts to the core of our being. All other words merely lie on the surface of our lives. They massage our egos or tickle our fancies. But truth bears down and penetrates into the depths of our very hearts. Truth cuts to the bone. When we are pierced by the truth, it opens us up and allows us to see ourselves as God sees us.

Truth is so powerful, that it alone can save us from the wrath to come. Truth can sanctify us into the image of Jesus Christ. Truth has the power to strengthen the weak. It encourages the downcast. It guides the lost. It challenges the sluggish. It comforts the discouraged. Truth does what only God can do because it is the truth of God Himself.

Truth Determines Destinies

Eighth, truth is *determinative.* Your relationship to the truth charts the course of your life in this world. It defines how you will love your spouse, how you will raise your children, and how you will direct your business. The truth is a lamp unto your feet and a light unto your path. Truth is so determinative that your entire being is marked by the truth. Ultimately, truth will have the say on whether you spend eternity in heaven or in hell. Your final destiny is determined by the truth.

By these attributes of the truth, we can discern its true nature. All that is not in alignment with the truth is at best in error and at worst a lie. We live in a day in which the world largely rejects the truth. As a result, we must clearly understand what the truth really is. As Jesus stood before Pilate, boldly testifying to the truth, we understand that we, who belong to Him, must likewise boldly stand for the truth as well. We must affirm the truth for the glory of God and the salvation of those around us.

The Reign of Truth

Pontius Pilate defiantly rejected the truth when he mocked, "What is truth?" This was in response to the words spoken by Jesus that had affirmed the certain reality of truth: "For this purpose I was born and for this purpose I have come into the world—to bear witness to the truth." Then, Jesus affirmed the reign of truth when he said to Pilate, "Everyone who is of the truth listens to my voice" (John 18:37). Here Jesus spoke about the reign of the truth in the hearts of men and women. If all people have an aversion to the truth, how does anyone receive the truth? Why do some accept the truth? Jesus explains in these words.

In no uncertain terms, Jesus stated that those who are "of the truth" will hear His voice. To be "of the truth" means to be spiritually birthed by the truth of the saving gospel of Jesus Christ. This describes those who have been regenerated by the truth. They are those who have believed the truth and belong to the truth because they have been birthed by the truth. That is to say, they have been sovereignly regenerated by the Spirit of truth. The Apostle Peter wrote, "You have been born again, not of perishable seed but of imperishable, through the living and abiding word of God" (1 Peter 1:23). The Word of Truth is the instrument that God uses to impart new life to the spiritually dead soul.

By this work of sovereign grace, God gives spiritual eyes to those who are blinded by sin in order to see the truth. God gives spiritual ears to hear the truth. He gives a new mind to understand the truth. He gives a new heart to receive the truth. God placed the Holy Spirit within us as His resident truth Teacher to guide us into all the truth. Jesus said that this is the case for everyone who is of the truth. There are no exceptions to this reality. The reception of the truth of God is necessary if it is to save and sanctify any person's life.

To be "of the truth" describes those who have received the effectual call of God. This, in turn, has caused the truth of the gospel to be received and believed. God sovereignly draws His own by the power of the Holy Spirit so that the truth will break into their hearts with irresistible force. Suddenly, they are enabled to see the spiritual truths to which they were previously blind and against which they were hardened. It is the work of God the Holy Spirit that causes one to hear the voice of the Lord Jesus Christ and to follow Him.

Ears to Hear the Truth

Jesus said, "My sheep hear my voice, and I know them, and they follow me. I give them eternal life, and they will never perish, and no one will snatch them out of my hand. My Father, who has given them to me, is greater than all, and no one is able to snatch them out of the Father's hand. I and the Father are one" (John 10:27–30). The sheep hear the voice of Christ, while the goats remain deaf to this call. Mankind is entirely dependent upon the Giver of all truth to impart His truth to the human soul.

As we live in this world full of lies with people around us saying, "What is truth?" we who are of the truth know that Jesus came into this world to testify to the truth. The truth testified to us and set us free. Apart from the truth, people will remain bound in their sin. Only the truth of God is powerful enough to unlock the iron chains that imprison man and set him free.

These three major themes—the rejection of truth, the reality of truth, and the reign of truth—are seen in this encounter between Jesus and Pilate. They are likewise seen as we live in the world. We see the rejection of truth on a daily basis, whether in the world or, more surprisingly, within the church.

The reality of truth calls us today through the living and active Word of God that bears witness to the gospel message concerning our eternal destiny. The truth, the whole truth, and nothing but the truth—this is our most noble pursuit in this world.

2

YOUR WORD IS TRUTH

The Reality of Truth in the Inerrant Word

When Martin Luther was summoned by Holy Roman Emperor Charles V to appear before the imperial diet in Worms, Germany, in April 1521, he was to stand at his own heresy trial in which he would be called upon to recant his writings. Despite the warnings of friends not to appear, Luther nevertheless traveled from Wittenberg to Worms, preaching in the villages and towns along the way, believing that the truth would win the day.

At Worms, the political and ecclesiastical hierarchy gathered with the intent to expose Luther as a heretic. The prosecutor, Johann Eck, representing the Church of Rome, pressed Luther with two questions as the books he had written lay on the table before him. The first question was simple enough: "Martin Luther, are these your books?" Then came the second question that was far more significant: "Will you recant?" Sensing the magnitude of the moment, Luther asked for a recess and retired for the evening. He reappeared the next day and spoke those now-famous words that are a trumpet blast in the ear of every true believer:

> Unless I am convicted by Scripture and plain reason—I do not accept the authority of popes and councils, for they have often contradicted each other—my conscience is captive to the Word of God. I cannot and I will not recant anything, for to go against conscience is neither right nor safe. God help me. Amen.[1]

Standing for the Truth

That definitive stand for the Word of God proved to be the shot heard around the world. By this bold assertion, Luther declared that the Bible holds the highest authority in the life of the church. He maintained that the Scripture is supreme over popes and councils. This was the public declaration of what would soon become known as *sola Scriptura*, Latin for "Scripture alone." The Roman Catholic Church had espoused that the truth lay in the Scripture *and* tradition, Scripture *and* ecclesiastical councils, and Scripture *and* the pope—always Scripture plus something or someone else. But Luther courageously took the contrary stand upon Scripture alone.

At each point of the ensuing controversy, Luther remained unwavering in his commitment to the Scripture alone. He proved to be a modern-day Athanasius, standing *contra mundum*, "against the world." This immovable monk stood as one man against the

---

1. Roland H. Bainton, *Here I Stand: A Life of Martin Luther* (Nashville, Tenn.: Abingdon, 1950), 182.

entire religious and political world, with its one thousand years of dead tradition. Luther said, "I bear upon me the malice of the whole world, the hatred of the emperor, of the pope, and of all their retinue. Well, on in God's name; seeing I am come into the lists, I will fight it out."[2] Luther was like an ice-breaker ship that plowed the frozen tundra of his generation, allowing the rest of Europe to follow behind him.

Luther maintained a strong stance on the Scripture, even though it meant a death sentence placed upon his head. He courageously declared, "From the year of our Lord 1518 to the present time, every Maundy Thursday at Rome I have been by the pope, excommunicated and cast into hell, and yet I live. This is the honor and crown we must expect and have in this world."[3] In other words, to stand publicly for the truth of God and suffer for it is a badge of honor in discipleship. Jesus said that a servant is not above his master. If they persecuted the Lord, they will persecute believers who stand up for the truth taught in the Word of God.

The Truth Crisis

Like Luther five hundred years ago, we live in a time of crisis over the truth. We are witnessing an aggressive assault on the Scripture on every side as liberal denominations and apostate seminaries are attacking the inerrancy of the Bible. Modernism and pragmatism are attacking the sufficiency of Scripture by insisting that human

---

2. Martin Luther, *Table Talk* (Orlando, Fla.: Bridge-Logos, 2004), 260.
3. Ibid., 258.

wisdom must supplement divine wisdom. The emerging church assails the perspicuity of Scripture, claiming that the Bible cannot be understood with certainty. Charismatics and noncessationists assault the finality of the Bible by adding supposed mystical revelations to the closed canon of the Scripture. The cults attack the very message of the Word of God, distorting the person and work of Jesus Christ. Rome still attacks the singular authority of the Bible, adding its tradition, ecclesiastical councils, and papal decrees. On and on, the attacks continue to pound like the endless waves of the ocean against the shore, rising up and foaming in their opposition against the singular authority of the Word of God.

Yet despite these aggressive assaults upon the Bible, this book remains an immovable rock of truth. The Scripture is an unassailable refuge for all who believe its claim to be the very Word of God. It is an impenetrable fortress that does not budge under the relentless attacks mounted against it. The Word of God stands as strong today as when it was first written. The man or woman who stands upon it can withstand every deception of the world. The Word of God is so strong that when we build our lives upon it by faith, we, too, cannot be swayed. As we are confronted with the many attacks upon the Bible, we must remain strong in the faith and say as Luther did, "Here I stand, I can do no other. God help me."

In this moment of truth, we must embrace and proclaim the reality of truth as recorded in the Word of God. In order to succeed in this endeavor, we must understand two truths: first, where we must stand, and second, why we must stand.

Where We Must Stand

There are six nonnegotiable truths upon which we must stand in regard to the Scripture. These truths are the inspiration, inerrancy, authority, perspicuity, sufficiency, and invincibility of the written Word of God. Herein is found the truth of God. It is in the Bible that we have the record of the special revelation of God, enabling us to be a force for Him in this world. The written Word of God is, the Apostle Paul said, "the word of truth" (2 Tim. 2:15) that contains "the message of truth" (Eph. 1:13, NASB). James affirmed it as "the word of truth" (James 1:18). Jesus stated, "Your word is truth" (John 17:17).

The Inspiration of Scripture

First, we must have confidence in the truth of the divine *inspiration* of Scripture. Every believer must be firmly convinced that the Bible is the inspired Word of the living God. The Apostle Paul writes, "All Scripture is inspired by God" (2 Tim. 3:16, NASB). The words "inspired by God" are one word in the original Greek (*theopneustos*), which means "God-breathed." From Genesis to Revelation, all Scripture is inspired by God, meaning it is breathed out of the mouth of God. Jesus said, "Man shall not live by bread alone, but by every word that comes from the mouth of God" (Matt. 4:4). In the truest sense, the doctrine of the inspiration of Scripture is the doctrine of expiration. That is to say, Scripture is breathed out by God. With the Bible, there is one primary Author (God) who used many secondary authors (men) to record its message. The human authors were simply the instruments in the hand of God to record the Scriptures. But there is only one primary Author, God Himself, who speaks to us through His Word.

The inspiration of Scripture extends down to its minutest detail. Jesus said, "For truly, I say to you, until heaven and earth pass away, not an iota, not a dot, will pass from the Law until all is accomplished" (Matt. 5:18). The smallest letter in the Hebrew language is a *yod*, similar to an apostrophe in the English language. It is like a thin eyelash, almost imperceptible to the naked eye. The smallest stroke in Hebrew is simply a little extension from a letter to distinguish one letter from another. It would be like differentiating a lowercase *l* from a lowercase *t*—just one line separates the two letters. Jesus said the Word of God will be accomplished down to the smallest stroke that would distinguish one Hebrew letter from another and to the smallest Hebrew letter in the entire alphabet.

As we open the Bible and read its message, it is not the wisdom of man that we are being taught, but the very mind of God being made known to us. The Scripture contains the wisdom of God that is able to make us wise unto salvation (2 Tim. 3:15). It is truth that has come down from the throne of God.

The Inerrancy of Scripture

Second, we must also uphold the truth of the *inerrancy* of Scripture. When the Bible speaks, it speaks pure, unadulterated truth without any mixture of error. It is impossible for the Word of God to contain any error or distortion of reality because it has proceeded from God Himself. Titus 1:2 asserts that "God . . . never lies." Any error or falsehood is impossible for God, who is perfectly holy in His being. Hebrews 6:18 affirms the same when it states, "It is impossible for God to lie." The Word of God is inseparably connected to His own nature. Simply put, a holy God cannot lie in His Word.

In Psalm 12:6, we see the inerrancy of Scripture confirmed: "The words of the LORD are pure words, like silver refined in a furnace on the ground, purified seven times." Precious metals are often found mixed with base metals, and so they were placed in a fiery furnace so that the heat would cause the impurities to separate from the silver or gold. The impurities would rise to the surface and be skimmed off the top, so that what remained was a pure, precious metal. Likewise, in this twelfth psalm, David is saying that the Scripture has been tested by God seven times, which is the number for perfection, so that there are no impurities in the Word of God. God has spoken exactly what is true in His Word. Scripture cannot contradict itself, and the Holy Spirit cannot contradict Himself. The result is the pure, unvarnished truth of Scripture.

The inerrancy of Scripture gives us great confidence that every truth taught in its pages is without any error or human reasoning. It is unmingled with any imperfections, but actually contains the perfect truth of God. Every word contains an accurate representation of reality, as things truly are.

The Authority of Scripture

Third, we must be in submission under the *authority* of Scripture. Because the Bible is the Word of God Himself, it speaks with the authority of God Himself. The Bible possesses the right to rule over our lives. Scripture is sovereign because God is sovereign. Thus, every knee must bow to the truth that is recorded within its pages. In Psalm 19:7, Scripture is identified as "the law of the LORD." The Bible is not a collection of suggestions from God; it does not give us options or preferences to consider. Instead, Scripture must be recognized as the authoritative law of God by which every life is directed to live.

In the day of Jesus, the Pharisees elevated their own traditions above the authority of the Word of God. The same thing occurred in the day of Luther, who understood that neither the pronouncements of the pope nor the word of any man could be elevated above the authority of Scripture. God's Word mediates the rule of God over the life of the church. Luther insisted, "Preachers must prove their claims with the word. When they extol the authority of the fathers and of Augustine, of Gregory and likewise of the councils, our answer is those things have no claim on us, we demand the word."[4] The German Reformer further noted, "Scripture alone is the true Lord and Master of all writings and doctrine on the earth. God's word must be supreme or nothing."[5] In other words,

4. *Luther's Works: Lectures on Genesis*, trans. Helmut T. Lehmann (St. Louis: Concordia, 1986), 9.

5. Martin Luther, *Defense and Explanation of All the Articles*, in *Luther's Works*, vol. 32: *Career of the Reformer II*, ed. Helmut T. Lehman (Minneapolis: Fortress, 1958), 11–12.

There is no moderating position on the Word of God. It is either sovereign over the life of every believer, or it is to be discarded as ancient myth.

It is the conviction of every believer that the Scripture is authoritative and rules over them with supreme authority. The Bible was not given to us to be interesting or stimulating. Rather, it was given to be arresting, that it would command our lives in order that we might please God.

The Perspicuity of Scripture

Fourth, we must further embrace the truth of the *perspicuity* of Scripture. The term *perspicuity* means that the Bible is written in accessible language with an accommodating style. In other words, it is understandable by ordinary people in essential matters of salvation and Christian living. Therefore, the Word is to be given to all people from all backgrounds. It is not to be withheld for the intellectual elite only. The Bible is the people's book—it is for all people, educated or uneducated, cultured or uncultured, religious or irreligious.

However, in the time of the Reformation, the leaders of the Roman Catholic Church considered the people to be too uneducated and untaught to understand the truth of Scripture. Therefore, the religious hierarchy kept the Word of God from the people, choosing instead to be the sole interpreters of the Word. But when Luther burst onto the scene, he declared that the Word of God is understandable and should be accessible to every man. He believed that an everyday workingman—a blacksmith or farmer—could take the Word of God and understand what God is saying. The father of the English Reformation, William Tyndale, said it was his goal that a plowboy in the field would know more of the Word of God than the pope in Rome.

This clarity of Scripture is what Psalm 19:8 refers to when it states, "The commandment of the Lord is pure" (NASB). This word "pure" means that God's Word is cogent, coherent, and unambiguous. The message of the Bible is not obscure or oblique. This fact was seen when Jesus appealed to the Pharisees with this question: "Have you not read that he who created them from the beginning made them male and female?" (Matt. 19:4). He asked elsewhere, "Have you never read in the Scriptures . . . ?" (Matt. 21:42). Have you not read about the resurrection of the dead? Had they not read in the law that on the Sabbath, the priest and temple break the Sabbath? In other words, Jesus indicated that the meaning of Scripture is plain enough to anyone who can read what it says.

In like manner, Luther insisted on the perspicuity of the Scripture: "No clearer book has ever been written on earth than the Holy Scripture. Everything in it has been brought into the most definite light and published to all the world."[6] He further said, "The meaning of Scripture is so certain, accessible, and clear, that it both interprets itself, as well as tests, judges, and illuminates everything else. It is such a bright shining light in a

6. Ewald M. Plass, *What Luther Says: An Anthology* (St. Louis: Concordia, 1959), sec. 222.

dark world, that we can see this light, and it gives us the light to understand everything else."[7]

The Sufficiency of Scripture

Fifth, we must also embrace the truth of the *sufficiency* of Scripture. Psalm 19:7 says, "The law of the LORD is perfect." This word "perfect" also means "whole and complete, lacking in nothing." In other words, Scripture is a comprehensive revelation of truth from God to man that is fully capable to carry out all His saving and sanctifying purposes. In Isaiah 55:11, God says of His Word, "It shall not return to me empty, but it shall accomplish that which I purpose, and shall succeed in the thing for which I sent it." Whatever God is doing on the earth, He is accomplishing it by His Word. No one is saved apart from the Word of God. Neither is anyone conformed to the image of Christ apart from the Word of God. Nor is anyone equipped for ministry apart from the Word of God. Everything good and eternal that God accomplishes in this world, He does by the execution of His Word.

The Apostle Paul notes that through Scripture, "The man of God may be complete, equipped for every good work" (2 Tim. 3:17). By the instrumentality of God's Word, man is made competent, capable, proficient, and adequately equipped for every good work assigned to him by God. Through Scripture,

---

7. Martin Luther, *Assertion against the Bull* (1520) in *WA* 7, 97, 23–24, cited in Bernhard Lohse, *Martin Luther: An Introduction to His Life and Work* (Minneapolis: Fortress, 1986), 157.

the believer is competent to counsel, able to evangelize, adept to comfort broken hearts, and sufficiently empowered to confront sinful lifestyles. In every ministry that God calls us to do, the Scripture equips us to fulfill it.

We need not look to any other book to explain the true human condition. No other philosophy or psychology book is needed to diagnose man's most basic problem, for no other book contains the solution to the human heart. A believer with a Bible will be able to make more of an eternal impact on the world than a general of a vast army. A believer equipped with only a Bible is ready to influence this world for eternity.

The Invincibility of Scripture

Finally, we must stand upon the reality of the *invincibility* of Scripture. No human weapon can match the supernatural power of the Word of God. No human heart can resist the Word of God when it is accompanied by the power of the Holy Spirit. In Jeremiah 23:29, God says, "Is not my word like fire, declares the LORD, and like a hammer that breaks the rock in pieces?" That is to say, the Scripture is able to melt down and purify even the most sinful heart. And the most hardened hearts will yield to the invincibility of the Word of God through the power of the Holy Spirit. The Word has power to convict, convert, cleanse, conform, console, counsel, and cheer.

Ephesians 6:17 says, "And take . . . the sword of the Spirit, which is the word of God." What an offensive weapon the Word of God is! Every piece of armor mentioned in this passage is a defensive piece of protection, except for the sword of the Spirit. We must unsheathe this sword in the power of the Spirit as we fight the good fight of faith.

Hebrew 4:12 speaks of the all-sufficient power of Scripture: "For the word of God is living and active, sharper than any two-edged sword." It is a living book that possesses the very life of God. When received by faith, the Bible is the means by which God imparts eternal life to the spiritually dead soul. The Word of God is also "active," which comes into the English language from the Greek word for "energy." The Word is full of divine energy and empowers human lives as it works. It is a powerful and effective instrument in the hands of any person. The word is able to pierce as far as the division of soul and spirit.

No instrument on earth is as powerful and as penetrating as God's Word. It is far sharper than any surgeon's scalpel. Every verse is razor sharp. Every text has a cutting edge to it. Every passage is a chef's knife. It can cut through every human facade, expose every human excuse, overcome every human resistance, and unmask every human pretense. Every human heart yields to this two-edged sword. It is not Scripture plus another message that has such power, but truly Scripture alone.

This is precisely where we must stand in this day. Either we stand upon Scripture alone, or we will be standing on sinking sand. We must put our full confidence in this super-natural word. As never before, mounting pressure is coming against us regarding what we believe and where we stand. We now find ourselves in a post-Christian society, no longer surrounded by people who hold our worldview or standard of authority. Now more than ever, we must be rooted and grounded in the Word of God, or we will find ourselves with no place to stand at all.

As we do, we must be willing to stand alone for the truth wherever God places us. This means you may be the only believer in your school, your office, your family, or your neighborhood. We must not cave in to the mounting pressures around us to conform to the majority. We cannot apologize for the faith once for all delivered to the saints. Though the winds of opposition howl all around us, we have a firm place to stand. It is that tree that is most deeply rooted and grounded in the fertile soil of Scripture that will be able to withstand the forces in the coming days. Let us encourage one another to stand strong where great men and women of the faith once stood, and find the stability we need.

Why We Must Stand

Having considered *where* we must stand in regard to the truth as found in the Scripture, we must also comprehend *why* we must stand uncompromisingly in our commitment to this truth. A proper motivation in Christian living is always a significant element of any believer's life. So let us consider why we should stand so resolutely on the Word of God.

Standing with God

First, we must stand firm for the truth of Scripture because to do so is to stand with its Author, God Himself. God and His written Word are inseparably bound together. As Augustine said, "When the Bible speaks, God speaks."[8] To abandon the Bible is to abandon God. As we saw in 2 Timothy 3:16, "All Scripture is breathed out by God." Scripture contains the very words that have proceeded from the mouth of God. So any departure from a firm commitment to the verbal, plenary inspiration of Scripture is a falling away from God Himself. Any group of people, whether it be a denomination, seminary, ministry, church, or pulpit, that departs from an unwavering stance on God's Word has begun the process of apostasy. This is always the first point of departure: a departure from the written Word.

Standing with Jesus

Second, we must stand strong for the truth of Scripture because it is necessary in order to stand with Jesus Christ. The written Word and the living Word are inseparably bound together. There are amazing parallels between the written Word and living Word. Consider the virgin birth of Jesus Christ. The Holy Spirit conceived in Mary's womb supernaturally so that she, a sinful woman, would bring forth the sinless Son of the living God. Likewise, the Holy Spirit powerfully moved upon sinful men in the writing of God's Word, so that they, sinful men, recorded the Word of God without any flaw or error. There is an intentional parallel between the written Word and the living Word, such that to deny the Word is to deny the Lord. To depart from the

8. Augustine, *City of God*, 3.8–11, trans. David. S. Wiesen (Cambridge, Mass.: Harvard University Press, 1968), XI.2.

written Word is to depart from the living Word. To forsake the one is to forsake the other.

Jesus Himself strongly asserted the full inspiration and flawless inerrancy of Scripture. He said, "Whoever relaxes one of the least of these commandments and teaches others to do the same will be called least in the kingdom of heaven, but whoever does them and teaches them will be called great in the kingdom of heaven" (Matt. 5:19). He also said in Matthew 24:35, "Heaven and earth will pass away, but my words will not pass away." Either Jesus is telling us the truth or Jesus is a liar. As C.S. Lewis said so well, He is either Lord, liar, or lunatic. Put another way, He is either deity, deceiver, or deceived. We know that a liar or a lunatic cannot be anyone's savior. If Jesus was wrong about Scripture, then He was also wrong when He said, "I am the way, and the truth, and the life" (John 14:6). To deny the truthfulness of what Jesus said would be to deny the sinlessness of the Lord Jesus Christ. Jesus and His Word are inseparably bound together, so that to deny the Word of God is to deny the Head of the church who speaks through His Word.

Standing with the Gospel

The final reason why we must stand firm upon the truth of Scripture is that to abandon the Word of God is to abandon the gospel. To depart from the authority of Scripture is to embark upon a path that abandons the only way of salvation. No one can be born again until the seed of holy Scripture is planted within the soul. Peter writes, "You have been born again, not of perishable seed but of imperishable, through the living and abiding word of God. . . . And this word is the good news that was preached to you" (1 Peter 1:23–25). Any compromise in a fundamental belief in the Word of God itself will compromise the reality of the new birth. No one can believe the gospel yet disbelieve the source of the gospel in the written Word.

The one who calls upon the name of the Lord must have full confidence in its message as recorded in Scripture. The Apostle Paul wrote:

> For "everyone who calls on the name of the Lord will be saved."
> How then will they call on him in whom they have not believed? And how are they to believe in him of whom they have never heard? And how are they to hear without someone preaching? And how are they to preach unless they are sent? As it is written, "How beautiful are the feet of those who preach the good news!" But they have not all obeyed the gospel. For Isaiah says, "Lord, who has believed what he has heard from us?" So faith comes from hearing, and hearing through the word of Christ. (Rom. 10:13–17)

No one can possess true faith in Jesus Christ and yet not believe the Bible itself.

For a New Reformation

J.H. Merle d'Aubigné, the great historian of the Swiss Reformation, wrote, "The only true Reformation is that which emanates from the word of God."[9] This certainly occurred in the sixteenth

9. J.H. Merle d'Aubigné, *History of the Reformation of the Sixteenth Century*, vol. 5: *The Reformation in England* (New York: American Tract Society, 1847), 149.

century in the Protestant Reformation. That movement was marked by a decisive return to the authority of the Word of God. If we are to see another great work of God in these days, we must stand firmly on *sola Scriptura*. The Reformation, the First Great Awakening, and every other true revival in the annals of church history were ushered in by a return to full confidence in the Word of God. God will honor the people who honor His Word.

If we are to see such a new reformation in our day, our churches must fully embrace every aspect of the truth of Scripture. With renewed devotion, pastors must become fiercely committed to proclaiming the full counsel of God while denying any error that contradicts the written Word. Elders must govern the church by Scripture alone. Every tradition in the church must yield to the authority of Scripture. While many church traditions are rooted and grounded in biblical truth, those that are contrary to the Word of God must submit to the higher authority of Scripture. Our worship services must be regulated by the Word of God, for it matters to God how we worship Him. As John Calvin said, "Let them do all according to the word of God."[10]

Any effective witness of the church in the world must be done according to the Word of God, in order to set forth the Word of God. A worldly message will never win the world to faith in Jesus Christ. Instead, God will honor only those who honor His Word. Whether preacher, housewife, businessman, or student, we must stand firm on the truth of God as infallibly

10. John Calvin, *Sermons on the Epistle to the Ephesians* (Edinburgh, Scotland: Banner of Truth, 1973), xii.

recorded in the Scripture. Moreover, we must be willing to enter into conflict for the truth. We must be ready not only to state what is true but to refute what is error.

As Luther found himself in the turmoil of the Reformation, people came to him and asked him how all this had happened. How was Europe now teetering and tottering? How was the pope now beginning to shake? How had a match been lit that set the world ablaze? Luther responded, "I simply taught, practiced, preached, and wrote God's Word. Otherwise I did nothing. And while I slept . . . , the Word so greatly weakened the papacy, that never a prince and never an emperor inflicted such damage upon it. I did nothing. The Word did it all."[11] It was this firm commitment to the truth that ignited the fires of the Reformation in his day.

In our moment of truth, our confidence in the truth can be no less. Let us go into the highways and byways, spreading the Word of God far and wide. Then let us also go to sleep, as Luther suggested, trusting that the Word will do its work. As we witness God causing His Word to spread and prosper, let us also say, "I did nothing. The Word did it all."

---

11. Martin Luther, "Second Wittenberg Sermon (1522)," in *Works of Martin Luther*, ed. Henry Eyster Jacobs (Philadelphia: Muhlenberg, 1943), 2:399.

3

BELIEVABLE TRUTH

The Reality of Truth in the Written Word

Why do you believe that the Bible is what it claims to be—the very Word of God? Why do you believe it is not merely another book? Why are you convinced that the Scripture is divine revelation? For what reasons do you believe the Bible is a supernatural book? The significance of these questions cannot be overstated. You cannot be wrong here and be right with God.

I want us to consider several objective reasons why the weight of evidence supports the reality that the Bible is the inspired, infallible Word of God. There are sufficient grounds for our faith to rest securely in the truth as recorded in Scripture. Our faith in the divine authorship of the Bible is not a blind leap in the dark. Such confidence is not based upon mere religious feelings. Nor is our faith in the written Word of God based upon sentimental emotions. To the contrary, there is a sturdy foundation of evidence that undergirds our belief that the Bible is indeed the Word of Truth.

From a divine perspective, we believe that the Bible is God's Word because its Author, the Holy Spirit, has borne witness to our human spirit that this Book contains the infallible truth of the living God. It is the Holy Spirit who has convinced us of the veracity of Scripture by bringing to our hearts His inward testimony, which persuades us that this Book is like no other book in the world. It is the Holy Spirit who convinces us that this is God's Book.

Nevertheless, this does not preclude rational reasons for holding this conviction. There are many intellectual evidences and convincing proofs that the Bible is God's Word. Our faith is built upon credible, objective facts, not merely subjective feelings or whims. The foundation of our Christian faith is the Bible, and there are many clear-cut, compelling reasons why we believe it is what it claims to be—the written Word of God. This step of faith in the divine authorship of Scripture is a reasonable step. Every person should understand the rational arguments for believing that the Bible is from God. Our convictions must rest upon strong pillars of truth that uphold our fundamental belief that the Bible is the Word of God.

In this chapter, we will explore a series of convincing arguments for why we should believe the Bible is the divine Word. These solid pieces of evidence serve as a reference points that then bolster our confidence in the Bible. Each line of reasoning should remind us why we are persuaded that the Bible is the written Word of the living God.

The Direct Claims of the Bible

First, we start at the most basic level, namely, we believe that the Bible is the Word of God because of its own direct claims. The Bible is authoritative in all subjects that it addresses, and this includes its own testimony about itself. In no uncertain terms, the Bible states that it is the very Word of God. When a defendant is brought into a courtroom, he is allowed to testify for himself. The same should be true for the Bible in the court of human opinion. We must allow the Bible to take the witness stand and give its own witness concerning itself.

The Apostle Paul states, "All Scripture is breathed out by God" (2 Tim. 3:16). These four words, "breathed out by God," come from one Greek word, *theopneustos*. It is a compound word formed of *theos*, meaning "God," and *pneustos*, meaning "breath or spirit." Therefore, *theopneustos* means "God-breathed," indicating that God Himself breathed out the Scriptures as it was recorded by its human authors. This verse does not say that God inspired the authors. Rather, the Scripture itself is inspired as it was breathed out of the mouth of God. The human writers were moved by the Holy Spirit (2 Peter 1:21) so that they recorded what God desired. Scripture is not the word of men, or any culture or society, but the direct product of divine authorship.

Thus Says the Lord

More than two thousand times in the Old Testament, we read statements like "Thus says the Lord," "the Lord said," "the word of the Lord came to me saying," "the law of the Lord," or "the precepts of the Lord." Again and again, we read these explicit claims by Scripture to be the Word of God. When we come to the New Testament, we read verses that are equally emphatic. For example, 1 Thessalonians 4:15 says, "For this we declare to you by a word from the Lord." The biblical authors were aware that their message did not originate within themselves. Nor was it collected from the culture or society. Rather, what these authors taught came down as a transcendent message from heaven. In 1 Corinthians 11:23, we read, "For I received from the Lord what I also delivered to you." Simply put, Paul acknowledged that what he wrote had been received from God.

Moreover, when we compare Old Testament verses with those in the New Testament, what God says in the Old Testament is often recorded as Scripture in the New Testament. In other words, the authors of the New Testament recognized the Old Testament to be Scripture. They believed that God speaks in both Testaments with one voice. The voice of God in the Old Testament is the same voice in the New Testament. Augustine and Calvin both said, "When the Bible speaks, God speaks." This is where we begin—the direct claims of Scripture that it is the Word of God.

The Perfect Unity of the Bible

Second, the perfect unity of the Bible also testifies to its divine origin. The more we study the Bible, the more we are impressed with its amazing unity amid its extraordinary diversity. The wide range of diversity in the Scripture is seen in the fact that it is made up of sixty-six different books, written over a period of almost 1,600 years, by over forty different authors, on three different continents, in three different languages. Consider the diverse background of these authors: two were kings, three were priests, one was a physician, two were fishermen, two were shepherds, one was a former Pharisee, two were statesmen, one was a tax collector, one was a military general, one was a scribe, one was a cupbearer, and one was a goat herder.

Moreover, consider the broad diversity of the literary genres with which they wrote. The Bible is written in narrative, poetry, prophecy, proverb, parable, discourse, gospel, epistle, allegory, song, legal writings, and more. There is also a wide-ranging diversity of the geographical locations from which they wrote: the Sinai desert, the palace of Jerusalem, a cave in Judea, the palace of Shushan, beside the River of Babylon, the land of Egypt, Macedonia, Greece, Rome, and Aberdeen Island (known as Patmos). Further, one can see the extensive diversity of its many parts, including almost three thousand different cast members in the storyline of the Bible, spanning some 1,189 chapters, comprising some 3,100 verses, requiring 700,000 words, containing 3.5 million letters.

Yet despite this complex diversity, the Bible speaks with a perfect unity that defies human explanation other than to conclude that the Bible is the Word of God. It comes together perfectly as one Book, written by one Author. The Scripture teaches one plan of salvation, one people of God, one story of human history, one problem of mankind, one solution for this problem, one standard of morality, one design for the family, and one chief object of its message. The Word of God speaks with one voice, never once contradicting itself. How can we account for this flawless unity in the midst of such vast diversity? The only reasonable explanation is that there is one Author who stands behind the Bible, and that Author is God Himself.

No Mere Coincidence

To illustrate, suppose every state in the Union were asked to excavate some of its natural stone, box it in a crate, put it on a railroad car, and send it to the nation's capital. Some states would send crates containing limestone, some states would send marble, some states would send sandstone, and other states would send granite. Once the trains arrived in Washington, D.C., they would be uncrated and brought together. The stones would be different sizes and shapes. Some would be square, some rectangular, some cubic, and some cylindrical. As they are brought together, all of the stones would interface perfectly and construct a replica of the Jefferson Memorial with its domes, side walls, buttresses, and arches, with no gaps, no flaws, and nothing missing.

How would we account for such unity? The only reasonable explanation is to conclude that there was a master architect overseeing the entire project who sent out specific measurements for what he desired and flawlessly administered the execution of the project to ensure that all of the pieces fit together perfectly. So it is with the Word of God. Every doctrine, every truth, every principle, every practice, and every standard of ethics fits together perfectly to form one temple of truth, the written Word of the living God. Not to believe this would be synonymous with believing that an explosion in a print shop could cause all of the letters to land on the ground and form the Oxford English Dictionary, without a mistake, in perfect alphabetical order. Do you think that would just happen? Absolutely not. In like manner, the Bible speaks with one voice on every issue that it addresses. Consequently, we should have the greatest confidence that this Book is the inspired Word of the living God.

The Reliable Transmission of the Bible

Third, we can confidently believe that the Bible is the divine Word because of the reliable transmission with which it has been passed down through the centuries. The Bible has come to us with far greater care and precision than any other book of antiquity. Until recently, the oldest known Hebrew manuscript of any length did not date from earlier than the first part of the tenth century after the time of Christ. That constituted a gap of some 1,300 to 1,400 years from the time of the writing of the last book of the Old Testament to the oldest copy of the Old Testament that we have. Then, in 1948, a little shepherd boy in the northwestern area of the Dead Sea picked up some stones and threw them into a cave, when he heard a thud. He walked into the cave and discovered one of the great archaeological treasures of modern history: the Dead Sea Scrolls.

Over the following months, archaeologists went into eleven different caves and found in them a treasure that had been hidden for some two thousand years—ancient copies of the original text of Scripture. There were discovered two copies of Isaiah, entire copies of Psalms and Leviticus, and thousands of fragments of different sections of the Old Testament. When Hebrew scholars began to piece these manuscripts together, our oldest copy of the Old Testament was instantly pushed back a millennium, virtually back to the days of the first-century church. What they learned was simply astonishing: over those thousand years, the transmission of the Word of God had been passed down with extraordinary accuracy.

No Other Book like It

There is no other book of antiquity that has been so carefully passed down to us than the Bible. The New Testament is even more remarkably preserved. We have almost six thousand early Greek manuscripts of the New Testament, and another ten thousand copies in the Latin Vulgate, to say nothing of Syriac and other Semitic languages. This large body of manuscripts substantiates the reliability of the transmission of the Word of God even throughout the entire copying process.

When we compare this with other ancient books written at the same time, the results are astonishing. For example, the poet Homer lived in 800 BC, and the time lapse between the time of his writing and the oldest known copy is some four hundred years. For the ancient philosopher Plato, the time gap is 1,300 years. For Julius Caesar and his writings, there is a span of a thousand years. Moreover, many of these ancient works are known to us through only a handful of surviving copies. But when we come to the New Testament, the earliest copies that we have date a mere fifty years after their writing. The earliest copy of an entire New Testament has a gap of only some two hundred years from its writing, and there are not simply six or seven copies of it, but some six thousand copies. The confidence that we should have in the reliability of the Bible that has been passed down to us is unsurpassed for any ancient book in any field of writing.

The Historical Accuracy of the Bible

Fourth, we believe that the Bible we hold in our hands is the written Word of the living God because of the confirming evidence of its historical accuracy. For example, take the historical accuracy with which Luke wrote his gospel and the book of Acts. In a work titled *The New Testament Documents: Are They Reliable?* British scholar F.F. Bruce writes that one of the most remarkable evidences of the historical accuracy with which Luke wrote is his familiarity with the proper titles of notable persons mentioned in his writings. This was by no means an easy feat in his day. Rather, this would have taken painstaking hours of laborious research, since there were no convenient reference books available by which he could gather this information. Bruce goes on to discuss that in the book of Acts, Luke is also geographically accurate at every point without having an atlas in front of him. Further, he addresses the various titles of Roman officials with absolute perfection.

Bruce argues that this would be similar to a new student arriving at Oxford University and, on his very first day on campus, being able to address everyone on the faculty and higher administration by their proper titles—provost, master, rector, and president. In Luke's day, many of the original Roman leaders were moving up the ladder, and their titles were constantly changing. Yet every time that Luke records them, he does so correctly without any historical mistakes. Surely, this accuracy points to the supernatural inspiration of the Bible.

The Archaeological Accuracy of the Bible

The more archaeologists dig in the Middle East and uncover artifacts, they are not finding evidence that reveals mistakes in the Bible. To the contrary, what they are discovering actually confirms the historical accuracy of the Bible. For example, they have uncovered the Pool of Bethesda mentioned in John 5:2, which was claimed by liberal scholars for many years to have never existed. However, archaeologists dug into the dirt in Jerusalem, and what do you suppose they discovered? The archaeologists unearthed what the Bible had recorded long ago—the Pool of Bethesda. Archaeology is not disproving the Bible, but the very opposite—confirming the reliability of Scripture.

Similarly, the first five books in the Bible—Genesis, Exodus, Leviticus, Numbers, and Deuteronomy—were assaulted by liberal scholars who argued that no written language was in use at the time that would have allowed someone to write the Pentateuch. Yet archaeologists discovered not only that Moses was able to write using the language of the day, but there was also a postal system in use that allowed people to exchanged letters. Simply put, there has never been a book of antiquity with the archaeological accuracy of the Bible.

The Scientific Accuracy of the Bible

Fifth, a fundamental belief in the Bible as the Word of God is validated as we consider its scientific accuracy. This is what we would expect of a book that claims to be God-breathed. We would expect every subject that it addresses to be recorded with flawless precision. For example, Genesis 1:1 says, "In the beginning, God created the heavens and the earth." Herbert Spencer, a famous scientist who died in 1903, announced that everything in the universe fits into one of five categories: time, force, action, space, and matter. This is all contained in the first verse of the Bible. "In the beginning [time] God [force] created [action], the heavens [space], and the earth [matter]."[1] In the first verse of the Bible, there is a scientifically accurate statement that accounts for everything that exists.

---

1. Cited in John MacArthur, *Nothing but the Truth: Upholding the Gospel in a Doubting Age* (Wheaton, Ill.: Crossway, 1999), 71.

For many years, stargazing scientists in the past sought to count the number of the stars in the heavens. Two centuries before Christ, an early astronomer named Hipparchus (c. 190–120 BC) looked up into the skies and counted the number of stars. He claimed there are 1,022 stars in the universe. Four centuries later, a mathematician named Ptolemy (c. AD 100–170) said that Hipparchus miscounted—there are actually 1,056 stars. Then subsequently, a German-born astronomer named Johannes Kepler (1571–1630), writing 1,500 years later, accounted for 1,055 stars. That was the recognized standard of the day in the scientific world of advanced learning.

But in 1610, the Italian astronomer Galileo Galilei (1564–1642) invented the telescope, and everything changed. He put it up to his eye and looked into the sky above, and what he saw brought him to his knees. He observed that there is an inestimable number of stars in the heavens. In fact, there are 100 billion stars—10 to the 24th power. But what had the Bible said all along? We read, "The host of heaven cannot be numbered" (Jer. 33:22). Once again, the Bible was correct, and the world of science was catching up to what God recorded long ago in His Word.

Scripture Trumps Science

We need to understand that the Bible is never catching up with science, but the scientific world is always catching up with the Bible. The Bible is true in all matters that it affirms, even science. There was a time when it was believed that the earth was flat, and if one sailed through the Strait of Gibraltar, he would go over the edge of the earth. There was no concept of the world's being a round globe. Yet 2,700 years ago, Isaiah recorded in Isaiah 40:22, "It is he who sits above the circle of the earth." The Word of God identifies this terrestrial ball in which we live as a circle. How did Isaiah know this? The answer is, holy men of God spoke and wrote as they were moved by the Holy Spirit (2 Peter 1:21).

For many years, it was believed by educated people that the earth rested on the shoulders of the Titan Atlas. This explanation pacified mankind until someone said, "What is Atlas standing on?" Someone replied, "Well, Atlas is standing on an elephant." Then someone asked, "What's the elephant standing on?" And they replied, "Well, the elephant is standing on a sea of snakes," and on and on it went. Yet Job 26:7 says, "He stretches out the north over the void and hangs the earth on nothing." Job lived some six thousand years ago and was likely a contemporary of Abraham. How could Job have known and recorded this scientific fact? The answer is that the Bible is the inspired Word of the living God and contains only the truth—for it is the Word of Truth.

Why do we not open the Bible and find inaccurate scientific statements, reflecting the thinking of the ancient day, that have been long since disproven? Why do we not read the Bible asserting that the earth is flat? Why do we not read that the earth is resting on an elephant? The answer is that all Scripture is divinely inspired and contains only the truth of God.

The Fulfilled Prophesies of the Bible

Sixth, the Bible confirms its divine origin by the fulfilled prophecies recorded in its pages. We could easily affirm that the Bible is the Word of God solely based on these pieces of evidence alone. Do you realize that at the time the Bible was written, 27 percent of it was prophetic? This is a staggering portion. A prophecy is prewritten history based upon the fact that only God knows the future because He alone has foreordained it. God is not looking down the tunnel of time to learn anything. He already knows everything. God has foreordained everything, and He recorded some of it in the Scripture.

We read the prophecy that Cyrus of Persia would become a ruler in Persia more than one hundred years before he assumed the throne (Isa. 45:1). Could you predict the name of the president of the United States one hundred years from today? This would be an entirely impossible feat for any one of us. But the Bible gave the name of this ruler long before he was even born. This fact gives us strong authentication of the Bible as the Word of God.

The most amazing fulfillments of prophecy are found in the first coming of Jesus Christ. It was prophesied in the Old Testament that Jesus would be born as the seed of Abraham, Jesse, and David. It was prerecorded in Scripture, centuries before His arrival, that He would be born in Bethlehem (Mic. 5:2). Further, He would be born of a virgin, and His name would be called Immanuel (Isa. 7:14). Great people would come to adore Him. He would be called out of Egypt (Hos. 11:1).

He would be preceded by a forerunner (Isa. 40:3–4). He would be anointed with the Holy Spirit (Isa. 11:1–3; 61:1–2). He would be a prophet like Moses (Deut. 18:15) and a priest after the order of Melchizedek (Ps. 110:4). He would enter into His public ministry in Galilee (Isa. 9:1–2). He would enter publicly into Jerusalem while riding on a donkey (Zech. 9:9) and come into the temple (Mal. 3:1). He would live in poverty (Isa. 53:2), meekness (Isa. 42:2), tenderness, and compassion (Isa. 40:11; 42:3). He would preach with parables (Ps. 78:2), work miracles (Isa. 35:5–6), and bear reproach (Pss. 22:6; 69:7, 9, 20; Isa. 53:4, 7).

Moreover, it was prophesied that Jesus would be rejected by His Jewish brethren (Ps. 69:8; Isa. 63:3), and the Jews and gentiles would conspire together against Him (Ps. 2:1). He would be betrayed by a friend (Pss. 41:9; 55:12–14). His disciples would forsake Him (Zech. 13:7). He would be sold for thirty pieces of silver (Zech. 11:12), and that price would be given for a potter's field (Zech. 11:13). He would die with intense suffering (Ps. 22:14–15), His sufferings would be for others (Isa. 53:4–6), yet He would be silent under that suffering (Isa. 53:7). He would be struck on the cheek (Mic. 5:1). His visage would be marred (Isa. 52:14; 53:3). He would be spit upon and scourged (Isa. 50:6). Further, it was prophesied that the hands and feet of Jesus would be nailed to the cross (Ps. 22:16). He would be forsaken by God and cry out, "My God, my God, why have you forsaken me?" (Ps. 22:1). He would be mocked (Ps. 22:7–8). Gall and vinegar would be offered to Him (Ps. 69:21). Lots would be cast for His clothing (Ps. 22:18).

He would be numbered among the transgressors, yet intercede for His murderers (Isa. 53:12). He would die, but not a bone of His body would be broken (Ex. 12:46; Ps. 34:20). He would be pierced (Zech. 12:10). He would be buried with the rich (Isa. 53:9). His flesh would not see corruption (Ps. 16:10). He would be raised from the dead (Ps. 16:10; Isa. 26:19). He would ascend to heaven (Ps. 68:18) and be seated at the right hand of God the Father (Ps. 110:1).

All of these prophecies and more were recorded hundreds of years before Jesus entered this world. It should be noted that many of these prophecies were fulfilled through the actions of Jesus' enemies who stood to lose the most from their fulfillment. The statistical probability that all of these prophecies would be fulfilled in one person has been described in the following manner: The state of Texas is 801 miles from top to bottom, and about that same distance across. Imagine that Texas was filled up with silver dollars as high as a man's shoulders, and one silver dollar was marked. If a person were put in a helicopter flying over the state and randomly lowered, what are the odds that he would pick up that one silver dollar with his first selection? The statistical probability that these prophecies would be fulfilled in one historical figure, Jesus of Nazareth, is less than if he would put his hand on that one silver dollar the first time. Every one of these fulfilled prophecies concerning the first coming of Jesus Christ is a validation of the inspiration, infallibility, authority, and inerrancy of the Word of the living God.

The Lord's Testimony about the Bible

The seventh reason to believe that the Bible is the Word of God is the testimony of Jesus Christ to its divine origin. The consensus of historians is that the greatest man who ever lived is Jesus Christ. Even false religions acknowledge the greatness of the Lord Jesus Christ. Some even call Him a great prophet. As Christians, we believe He is more than a prophet; He is the very Son of God and the Son of Man, truly God and truly man, the God-man. James Montgomery Boice wrote that the most important reason for believing the Bible to be the written Word of God is the unmistakable teaching of Jesus Christ Himself, who held the Bible in highest regard.

Referencing Deuteronomy 8:3, Jesus said in Matthew 4:4, "Man shall not live by bread alone, but by every word that comes from the mouth of God." By this affirmation, Jesus was asserting that the Scripture has proceeded from the mouth of God. He believed that while the Bible was recorded by the pen of men, it was, in reality, revealed by God Himself.

Later, Jesus said in Luke 16:17, "It easier for heaven and earth to pass away than for one dot of the Law to become void." In other words, it would be easier for the whole universe to go out of existence than for one little marking on one little letter of one little word in the Bible to fail. By this, Jesus was affirming the uniqueness of the Scripture, claiming it could not fail and would endure throughout time and eternity.

What would you say are the four stories in the Old Testament most ridiculed by liberals, skeptics, and unbelievers?

If I had to guess, I would list them as follows: the historicity of Adam and Eve, a literal Noah and flood, a literal Sodom and Gomorrah that were totally destroyed by divine fire, and a literal fish that swallowed the prophet Jonah. It is noteworthy that during the earthly ministry of Jesus, when He was pressured by His enemies and critics, He affirmed all four of those stories as literally true. Jesus affirmed the permanency of marriage by citing God's design for Adam and Eve (Matt. 19:4–6). Jesus also said that His second coming would be like the days of Noah (Matt. 24:38–39), and the final judgment like that which fell on Sodom and Gomorrah (Luke 17:28–29). He confirmed His own resurrection as the sign of the prophet Jonah, who was three days and three nights in the belly of the sea monster (Matt. 12:39–41). Jesus affirmed His resurrection, His second coming, and the final judgment on the most controversial stories in the Old Testament.

In fact, Jesus put His arms around the entire Old Testament canon for us in Luke 11:51 when He said, "from the blood of Abel to the blood of Zechariah." The blood of Abel appears in Genesis, and the blood of Zechariah is in 2 Chronicles, which is the last book in the Hebrew Bible. This is a literary device known as an *inclusio*, which functions like bookends. It is like seeing from the Atlantic to the Pacific and what is implied in every grain of sand in between. Jesus affirmed the thirty-nine books of the Old Testament, and in John 16, He guaranteed the New Testament canon as well.

The Amazing Indestructibility of the Bible

Eighth, we have solid reason to believe the Bible is the Word of God because of its amazing indestructibility. Despite the repeated attempts by infidels and unbelieving minds to tear down the Bible, there it stands, as strong as the day it was first written. The Bible is not the book of this month or the book of the year—it is the Book of the ages. Isaiah 40:8 declares, "The grass withers, the flower fades, but the word of our God will stand forever."

In a world that is passing away, the Bible endures. No matter what has attacked it, Scripture stands forever. Kings have banned it, emperors have forbidden it, critics have assailed it, philosophers have denounced it, atheists have assaulted it, infidels have mocked it, and yet it stands. The French skeptic Voltaire (1694–1778), who was heavily influenced by the English agnostic philosopher John Locke (1632–1704), said centuries ago, "One hundred years from my day there will not be a Bible on the earth except one that is looked upon by an antiquarian curiosity seeker."[2]

Fifty years after Voltaire's death, the Geneva Bible Society purchased his house, moved in their printing presses, and began to print the Word of God. They stocked Bibles all the way to the ceiling until no one could even enter the house. Two hundred years later, on Christmas Eve 1933, the British government paid the Russian government $510,000 for one ancient copy of the Bible, and on the very same day, a first edition of Voltaire sold

---

2. Cited in Mark Koval, "Enlightenment, Age of (Voltaire)," in *Encyclopedia of Time: Science, Philosophy, Theology, and Culture*, vol. 1, ed. H. James Birx (Los Angeles: SAGE, 2009), 420.

for eleven cents on the streets of Paris. Where is the wise man of this age? Where is the debater of this world?

The fact is that the Word of God is indestructible. This is exactly what the Bible claims of itself. Psalm 119:89 says, "Forever, O LORD, your word is firmly fixed in the heavens." Jesus said in Mark 13:31, "Heaven and earth will pass away, but my words will not pass away." This Book is indestructible, irresistible, inexhaustible, unquenchable, unconquerable, and uncontainable.

The Ethical Superiority of the Bible

Ninth, the transcendent moral code of the Bible provides further evidence of its divine origin. The Scripture contains a superior moral ethic that surpasses anything written in the ancient or modern worlds. Pagan religions were known for their disregard of human life, the family, and morality. False religions required their worshipers to sacrifice their babies to their idols. These cults worshiped in temples that were filled with prostitutes. But when we read the Bible, we see the total opposite.

The Scripture teaches the highest moral ethic ever recorded for man: "Honor your father and your mother. . . . You shall not murder. You shall not commit adultery. You shall not steal. You shall not bear false witness" (Ex. 20:12–16). We read in the Scripture, "Love your enemies"; "Love your wives"; "Do not provoke your children" (Matt. 5:44; Eph. 5:25; Col. 3:21). Think of all the common decency taught in the Bible: the sanctity of human life, racial equality, the dignity of women, good citizenship, social justice, legal equity, selfless service, individual integrity, and hard work. That which is right and decent and honorable is set forth in the Scripture and is confirmed in our own conscience. Surely, this high morality confirms the divine origin of the Bible.

The Supernatural Power of the Bible

Tenth, the supernatural power of the Bible is the final proof for its divine origin. The Scripture possesses the power to dramatically change any person's life who believes in Jesus Christ. The Word of God has divine power to sanctify, separate, purify, prune, convict, comfort, and guide our lives. Psalm 19:7–8 states: "The law of the LORD is perfect, reviving the soul; the testimony the LORD is sure, making wise the simple; the precepts of the LORD are right, rejoicing the heart; the commandment of the LORD is pure, enlightening the eyes." The Bible claims to be like a mirror that gives us true self-knowledge, enabling us to see ourselves for who we truly are (James 1:23). The Bible is represented as a sharp-edged sword that pierces as far as the division of soul and spirit (Heb. 4:12). It is pictured as a seed that contains the germ of life. The Bible is like a lamp unto our feet and a light unto our path (Ps. 119:105). The Bible is like a fire in our bones that consumes all that opposes it. It is like a hammer that breaks the rocks of unbelief to pieces (Jer. 23:29). The Bible is like milk that nourishes the soul (1 Peter 2:2).

No other book can tell us who we are, where we have come from, and where we are going. No other book makes the accurate diagnosis of our spiritual condition before God. The Word of God transforms drunkards into those who are sober. It transforms prostitutes into those who are pure. It changes thieves into those who are content. By the powerful working of the Bible, the prideful are humbled, the broken are restored, the weak are strengthened, and the fearful are emboldened. Martin Luther said, "This book is alive, it speaks to me, it has teeth, it runs after me, it has hands, it lays hold of me."[3] Even so, the Bible pursues each one who will open its pages and read its message.

Not Just Another Book

Is the Bible just another book? The weight of the evidence clearly substantiates the claim that this Book is the Word of Truth. It is the inspired, inerrant, infallible, sufficient, authoritative, immutable, and sovereign Word of God that reigns with mastery over our lives. One anonymous writer has put it this way:

> This book contains the mind of God, the state of men, the way of salvation, the doom of sinners, and the happiness of believers. His doctrine is holy. Its presets are binding. Its histories are truth. Its decisions are immutable. Read it and be wise, believe it and be safe, practice it and be holy. It contains light to direct you, food to support you, and comfort to cheer you. It is a traveler's map, the pilgrim's staff, the pilot's compass, the soldier's sword, and the Christian's charter. Christ is its grand subject, our good its design, and the glory of God its end. It should fill the memory, rule the heart, and guide the faith. Read it slowly, read it frequently, and

3. *The Table Talk of Martin Luther*, ed. Thomas S. Kepler (1952; repr., Mineola, N.Y.: Dover, 2005), 207.

read it prayerfully. It is a mine of wealth and health to the soul and a river of pleasure.[4]

Let us have great confidence in what the Bible says, for herein is found the absolute truth of God. God has spoken with words that are infallible and unmistakable. This Word was recorded by the prophets, sages, Apostles, and their associates, yet it contains the message of God to the human race. Let us not build our lives upon the shifting sand of men's opinions and cultural viewpoints. We must build upon the solid rock of divine truth as revealed in this book, the Bible.

4. Cited in Bill Bright, *Discover the Book God Wrote* (Wheaton, Ill.: Tyndale House, 2005), 28.

4

THE GOSPEL TRUTH

The Reality of Truth in the Exclusive Gospel

Standing at the very center of Christianity is Jesus Christ. Simply put, Christianity is about Christ. He is the sum and the substance of the Christian faith, the Alpha and the Omega, the beginning and the end. There is no Christianity outside of Him. Christianity is not a cause to join or a code to follow, but a Christ to follow. Christianity begins and ends with the supreme person of Jesus Christ. The heart of His mission in coming to this world was His sin-bearing death upon the cross. The substitutionary death of Christ for guilty sinners was His very purpose in coming into this world.

At the cross, Jesus Christ appeased the righteous anger of God toward all who would put their trust in Him. He propitiated the divine fury we rightfully deserved by taking that divine wrath upon Himself. Through His shed blood, Jesus atoned for our sins and reconciled sinful men to a holy God. He entered the slave market of this world and laid down His life to purchase everyone who would believe in Him. The cross is cherished by all followers of Christ, but, tragically, it remains folly and a stumbling block to the unbelieving world. While the truth of the gospel shines forth in unparalleled brilliance, this message is scorned and rejected by the world. The truth of the cross is despised by those in darkness as being uncouth, unrefined, and unsophisticated. This stiff-necked reaction to the cross is the reality of the world in which we live.

This blatant rejection of the ignominious death of Jesus Christ is nothing new. In the early years of Christianity, the Apostle Paul had to address this with the church at Corinth due to their compromise of the message of the cross. The death of Jesus Christ was being marginalized by the believers there, and Paul had to confront them about this tragic departure from the Christian faith. We find these words in 1 Corinthians 1:22–24: "For Jews demand signs and Greeks seek wisdom, but we preach Christ crucified, a stumbling block to Jews and folly to Gentiles, but to those who are called, both Jews and Greeks, Christ the power of God and the wisdom of God." This was the heart of the problem in the church at Corinth.

Through these divinely inspired words, God continues to give a strong warning to every church and believer. We must always hold the pure truth of the cross at the very center of our faith. The message of the cross of the Lord Jesus Christ must be the principle of truth that we hold high as we bear witness of the gospel of Jesus Christ.

The Influence of Athens

In order to understand why the Corinthian believers were in danger of watering down the message of the cross, we must realize that a mere forty-five miles from Corinth sat the influential city of Athens, home of the famous Greek philosophers, including Socrates, Plato, and Aristotle. The humanistic ideology that was birthed in Athens was making inroads into the church of Corinth. This worldly wisdom that promoted a man-centered worldview was establishing a beachhead in the Corinthian congregation. This secular philosophy was being brought into the church and diluting the message of the cross. As a result, the Apostle Paul penned the letter of 1 Corinthians to call the believers to refuse the message of the world and, instead, remain faithful to Jesus Christ and Him crucified.

Nothing has changed over the centuries. We certainly see this same secular encroachment into the church in our own day and age. Tragically, many churches so desire popularity in the world and growth in numbers that they have watered down the message of the cross. They have substituted the truth of the cross for a candy-coated message that bears no resemblance to the bloodstained crucifixion of Jesus Christ. The true gospel is always offensive to the world. What is sad is when this message becomes an embarrassment to the church and withheld from its preaching.

In 1 Corinthians, Paul confronted the church at Corinth by addressing how they had succumbed to the influence of the world by replacing the centrality of the cross with a more palatable message. These divinely inspired words were meant to confront the believers and call them to forsake their compromise of the gospel message. These ancient words still reverberate with relevance today for all believers who desire to uphold the reality of truth.

The Weakness of the Cross

Paul begins by noting that the world craves a palatable message that is devoid of the preaching of the cross. Both the religious crowd of the Jews and the secular audience of the Greeks saw no appeal in the cross. They instead wanted a message that was more appealing to their fleshly desires. Paul writes, "Jews demand signs and Greeks seek wisdom" (1 Cor. 1:22). This indicated that Jews desired a powerful display of miracles, not the apparent weakness of the message of the cross. At the same time, the Greeks wanted a profound new way of thinking about life, not the crude simplicity of the cross. To their carnal minds, the message of the cross failed to provide power for the Jews or profundity to the Greeks. Either way, the cross was sheer nonsense to both of these groups.

Paul first addressed the Jews by acknowledging, "Jews demand signs" (v. 22). The Apostle is referring to the first-century descendants of Abraham who had an outward form of religion but were inwardly devoid of saving grace. They were born Jews but had not been born again. They had a superficial knowledge of the Scripture but no saving knowledge of Jesus Christ. They were blinded by their own religious traditions, which kept them clothed in the filthy rags of their own self-righteousness.

The "signs" that these Jews wanted to see were a supernatural display of divine power in miracles. This would indicate that the kingdom of God was among them. Consequently, they craved a miracle-worker Messiah who had power over their military and political enemies. In the Old Testament, it had been prophesied that when the Messiah would come, He would usher in His kingdom with the display of miraculous power. The Jews wanted this miracle worker who could break the yoke of Roman oppression and return their national autonomy. They longed for a powerful leader who would restore the theocracy of Israel to its previous state under the kingly reigns of David and Solomon. The Messiah, they believed, would be a political champion who would usher in the sovereignty of the nation of Israel and make them premier among the nations.

However, these first-century Jews had no desire for a Savior who would deliver them from their own bondage to sin. Such was unthinkable. Other nations and peoples needed salvation from sins—not them. Neither did they desire a sovereign Lord who would rule over their lives. All they wanted was for the Romans to be under His rule. They longed to live as they once had done in an era of strength, autonomy, and independence. Consequently, the Jews saw no need for a Savior and Lord. They merely wanted a political leader who, by signs and miracles, would usher in a new day of political freedom and financial prosperity in their land.

So it is with many people today. In their eyes, the message of the cross is weakness that lacks the power to provide for their fleshly desires. They want a Jesus to make them healthy and wealthy. They want a Savior who will give them material riches and physical health. They want a Messiah who will make their nation strong again. But they do not desire a Savior with spiritual power to liberate them from their sins.

The Folly of the Cross

On the other hand, the Greeks in that day pursued "wisdom." They wanted an approach to life that placed the elevation of man in the center of all things. These Greeks were the well-educated and highly cultured gentiles, those who were looking for the latest philosophy and the newest perspective on life. In this context, "wisdom"—meaning the love of philosophy—refers to any worldly approach to life that draws upon humanistic philosophy. Wisdom is man's perspective on man's problems, offering man's solutions to promote man's agenda. That was exactly what the Greeks wanted. They searched for new ways to look at life, but they had no desire for the divine perspective on true wisdom. They had no appetite for God's wisdom revealed in the cross. Humble obedience to a crucified Jew was not on their agenda.

This rejection of the cross as foolishness is still with us today. This unbelieving world sees no wisdom in a Savior who died upon a cross many years ago. The crucifixion of Jesus Christ is a message of human weakness in their eyes, not divine brilliance. They have no desire to humble themselves under the lordship of Jesus. The message of the cross lacks panache in their eyes. There is no curb appeal in a crucified carpenter from Galilee.

The Primacy of the Cross

How did Paul respond to the craving of the worldly culture in Corinth? Did he capitulate and give the people what they wanted? After all, Paul was an Apostle who could perform miraculous signs. Further, he had been educated in the esteemed halls of academia with the finest human wisdom of his day. He had been trained at the feet of one of its great thinkers, Gamaliel. Paul was, undoubtedly, one of the most brilliant minds of the first century. Would Paul meet the culture at the point of their desires? Did he give them what they wanted in an attempt to win them over?

The Apostle Paul did not cave in to any of these base strategies. Instead, he responded by saying, "But we preach Christ crucified" (1 Cor. 1:23). Paul refused to perform signs or peddle worldly wisdom in order to lure a crowd into the church. For the Apostle, the end did not justify the means. He rejected the approach that would appeal to the worldly senses of his listeners, only to later introduce the cross through some kind of bait-and-switch tactic. He would not perform miraculous signs or pontificate on worldly wisdom to attract a crowd. To the contrary, he preached Christ crucified, which was the last thing the Jews and gentiles wanted to hear.

Death by crucifixion was the most shameful death known to man. A stigma was attached to anyone who died by this horrible death. In fact, crucifixion was so cruel and barbaric that no Roman citizen could be put to death upon a cross. It was simply too disgraceful. Only the worst criminals could be subjected to such a barbaric torture. Thus, the death of Christ was considered too shameful to mention publicly. Adding to the stigma of this public execution was the reality that Jesus probably died upon the cross that was prepared for a man named Barabbas. He was a notorious criminal, a terrorist who was the enemy of all that was good. The Greek world wanted a sophisticated message, but Paul proclaimed a graphic death on a bloody cross.

The Savior of the Cross

By Paul saying, "we preach Christ crucified" (1 Cor. 1:23), he meant that the primacy of his preaching focused upon Jesus Christ and Him crucified. All of the lines of his vast theology intersected at the sinless person and saving work of Jesus Christ. Certainly, Paul preached the full counsel of God (Acts 20:27). In his thirteen epistles in the New Testament, he taught on the broad diversity of every major area of theology. However, every aspect of his theology was centered in the person and work of Christ. Paul continually preached the glorious death of Jesus Christ upon the cross as the only way of salvation and sanctification.

The cross is the central truth of the Christian faith. The crucifixion of Christ is the doctrine that Paul relentlessly preached to the Corinthians. He would not be swayed to compromise and cheapen his message by adopting what either the Jews or the Greeks wanted. He adamantly refused to cater to the fleshly desires of the present culture. Martyn Lloyd-Jones, the great twentieth-century expositor at Westminster Chapel in London, was a physician before he entered into the ministry. Skilled in diagnosing his patients' problems, Lloyd-Jones said, "I never let the patient write the prescription." Lloyd-Jones refused to do this as a physician of the body, and neither would he allow the world to set his agenda in the church. Neither would he let it chart his course and craft his message on the diagnosis of the human soul. In like manner, we cannot allow the world's carnal clamoring to alter the message we preach.

The Offense of the Cross

The preaching of the cross of the Lord Jesus Christ inevitably results in conflict with the unbelieving mind. The word of the cross, Paul says, is "a stumbling block to Jews and folly to Gentiles" (1 Cor. 1:23). A "stumbling block" is what causes a runner to trip and fall headlong to his destruction. When Paul preached the truth of Christ and Him crucified to the Jews, he knew that it would be an offensive message. He knew it would cause them to be tripped up and fall. To them, Jesus was a lowly carpenter who lived for thirty years in obscurity. In their eyes, He was a religious fanatic who was followed by a band of nobodies for three years.

Worse, Jesus was condemned by Rome as a criminal and was crucified as an utter failure. In the Jews' eyes, Jesus died the most shameful death possible. How could their eternal destiny depend upon being rightly related to this crucified Christ? This crass message was an insurmountable stumbling block to the Jewish mind-set. What life could there possibly be in the humiliating death of this rejected nobody?

The Foolishness of the Cross

To the gentiles, the truth of the cross was no better. The Greeks saw the message of the cross as "folly." They wanted to hear a complex philosophical view of life that tickled their intellectual fancy. They wanted a message that would give them new insight into successful living. They sought intellectual stimulation concerning the real issues of life. The Greeks desired a sophisticated approach to life that addressed the fundamental perplexities of life: Who am I? Where have I come from? Where am I going? What is life all about? How can I find happiness? What is death? What is on the other side of death? Who is God? How does one know God?

The answer to all of these questions, Paul maintained, was to believe the simple gospel message of a crucified Jew who died upon a Roman cross. In their minds, this was sheer nonsense. In the Greek language, the word translated "folly" (*mōros*) is the root of the English word *moron*. In other words, the cross was moronic to them, sheer foolishness of the highest order. The gentiles perceived it to be madness, akin to spiritual insanity. To their refined, cultured sensitivities, only a fool would believe such a message.

The Sovereignty of the Cross

If the message of the cross is such a stumbling block and foolishness, how will any unbeliever see the wisdom and power of God in it? How will anyone believe if the gospel is so unappealing to the world? The Apostle Paul addresses these challenges when he adds, "but to those who are called, both Jews and Greeks, Christ the power of God and the wisdom of God" (1 Cor. 1:24). Those "called" are those who are chosen by God before time began (v. 27). It is predestined that all those chosen will be called and brought to faith in Jesus Christ (Rom. 8:29–30). This call is so powerful that it arrests the hearts of those to whom it is issued. This call apprehends the one called and draws him to faith in Jesus Christ. Those who are called will believe the truth of this message of grace.

The Apostle Paul will later explain why this divine call is so necessary. He writes, "The natural person does not accept the things of the Spirit of God, for they are folly to him, and he is not able to understand them because they are spiritually discerned" (1 Cor. 2:14). This statement clearly asserts that every unconverted person is spiritually blind and deaf, and, thus, cannot understand the gospel. It is as though preaching the gospel is describing a sunset to a blind man or a symphony to a deaf man. How does anyone believe its saving message? How will the preaching of the cross ever gain entrance into the hardened hearts of sin-blinded men and women? It will only come to pass as a result of the effectual call of God.

When Paul speaks of "those who are called," we must make a careful differentiation between the two calls in the Scripture as they relate to salvation. The first call is the general invitation that goes out to everyone who hears the gospel message. It is heard in the voice of the preacher by his listeners, or in the voice of parents by their children. This general call is heard in the witness of believers to their neighbors and work colleagues. This general call is extended whenever the truth of the gospel is made known and urges people to commit their lives to Christ. But whenever we invite someone to faith in Christ, we can only bring the message to their ears. We can go no further into the heart.

There must be another call that goes deeper into the soul. This is the special, saving call of God, known as the effectual call because it is truly always effective. This call always secures the result for which it is intended. This call is the powerful summons of God Himself that takes the gospel truth from the ear to the heart, where it is received by faith. Those who are called in this sense are the elect of God, those chosen by the Father before time began. At the appointed time, the Holy Spirit will call each one of these chosen ones out of the world and into a saving relationship with the Son of God, Jesus Christ (1 Cor. 1:9).

In 1 Corinthians 1:24, those who are the called are individually subpoenaed by God and brought to faith in Jesus Christ. As Christ crucified is preached, the Spirit calls these elect ones to faith in the Savior. Though the gospel is foolishness to Jews or a stumbling block to the gentiles, Christ is nevertheless building His church, and the gates of Hades cannot prevail against it.

The Provision of the Cross

There is only one way of salvation for both the Jew and the Gentile, and that is faith alone in Christ alone. To those who are called, Jesus becomes "the power of God" (1 Cor. 1:24). The cross is no longer perceived to be weakness, but power—the power of God to save. Jesus alone possesses the power to break the penalty of sin. He alone has the power to wash away the pollution of sin. And He alone has the power to triumph in grace in the lives of all who believe upon Him.

According to 1 Corinthians 1:30, three benefits flow from the wisdom of God in the cross, which are "righteousness," "sanctification," and "redemption." Each of these truths was drawn from the backdrop of various societal institutions in Paul's day. The word *righteousness* was drawn from the court of law, *sanctification* from the religious temple, and *redemption* from the slave market. Each of these terms reveals a different aspect of the accomplishment of Christ in His saving death upon the cross.

Righteousness represents the justification that is granted when we believe upon Jesus Christ. In this forensic act, God the Father imputes the perfect righteousness of Christ to the one who believes in Him. *Sanctification* speaks of the purifying work that occurs within our sin-stained souls as we are renewed through the work of the Holy Spirit and as we leave sinful patterns behind and walk in righteousness. *Redemption* expresses that upon the cross, Jesus paid the price for the wages of our sin and bought us out of the slave market of sin. Through

His atoning death, believers become the purchased possession of Jesus Christ.

The Wisdom of the Cross

Further, the preaching of the cross becomes "the wisdom of God" (1 Cor. 1:24) to those who are called. There is no greater display of the wisdom of God than in the cross of the Lord Jesus Christ. This gospel message was designed by the sovereign God of the universe who, in perfect wisdom and love, redeemed His people through the death of His Son. Though the cross is folly and a stumbling block to a depraved world, we must not compromise its truth. We must not change this message by cloaking it in the ways of the world in order to attract the world. In this moment of truth, believers must continue to preach Christ crucified in the face of much opposition and unbelief. The gospel is the only message that saves, and as we faithfully and lovingly bear witness of the cross of Christ, God the Spirit will draw the elect to Himself.

Paul was determined to preach Christ and Him crucified as the true wisdom that comes from God (1 Cor. 1:30). The greatest display of divine wisdom is seen in the cross of the Lord Jesus Christ. Only God, in His infinite genius, could have designed the profundity, yet simplicity, of the message of the cross. If we took counsel with all the brightest minds in human history, and they convened for ten thousand years, they never could have designed what God created in the saving cross of Jesus Christ. No human mind could have ever conceived that the second member of the Godhead would be born of a virgin, under the law, would meet all the requirements of the law, would bear our sins in His body upon the cross, and would impart perfect righteousness to all who would believe in Him. Only God in His infinite wisdom could have designed the saving message of Calvary's cross.

Nothing Has Changed

As believers, it is our responsibility to proclaim the divine truth in the gospel of Jesus Christ. We must spread this glorious gospel as far and as wide as we possibly can. There will be resistance and rejection from many in the world to whom this message is foolishness and folly. Yet in the midst of this unbelief, the sovereign purposes of God move forward as He sovereignly calls a chosen people to Himself. God will summon those who are His elect ones and then draw them into a saving relationship with His Son, Jesus Christ. Therefore, we must not do anything to diminish or compromise the truth of the cross.

To reach this lost world with the gospel, we do not need to adopt the foolishness of the secular message to enhance truth and make it more palatable. Paul makes it clear that if the truth is to be effective, it must first be offensive. Our duty is to bear witness to the truth that Jesus Christ has died for sinners as a perfect sacrifice for sins and trust God with the outcome. We are to issue the general call of the gospel to the whole world, and leave the results to God, who issues the effective call to those who are chosen. He brings them to repentance and faith in Jesus Christ.

There is salvation in no other name, for God has determined that salvation comes only through the death of His only begotten Son. There is not one drop of saving grace outside of the substitutionary death of the Lord Jesus Christ. He holds a monopoly on the grace of God for sinners. Jesus said, "I am the way, and the truth, and the life. No one comes to the Father except through me" (John 14:6). Only by faith in Jesus Christ is there deliverance from the wrath to come.

Part 2

THE REJECTION
OF TRUTH

5

WAR ON THE TRUTH

The Rejection of Truth by the First Couple

Since the dawn of human history, the truth of God has come under attack in every generation. We can trace this agelong conflict back to the beginning—to the perfect paradise of the garden of Eden. It was there that the avowed adversary of God, the devil, first slithered onto the stage of human history and launched a full-scale assault on the truth. Scripture clearly teaches that the truth has an unholy opponent, the devil, whose diabolical power is unleashed with great fury and force against it. However, many today deny the existence of a real devil. They have reduced him to the status of a mythological character. They recast him as a mere figment of man's imagination or as an innocent cartoon character.

These erroneous caricatures disregard what the Scriptures actually teach: that Satan is a real enemy of the truth. The Scripture is replete with teaching on the reality of Satan. He is explicitly named in seven books of the Old Testament and almost all of the books of the New Testament. The Lord Jesus Himself spoke clearly about the reality of Satan, including his evil character and work, and was even directly confronted by him in His temptation in the wilderness. In the Bible, this archenemy of God is known by many names: Satan, Lucifer, Beelzebub, Belial, Apollyon, the devil, the tempter, the ruler of this world, the god of this age, the prince of the power of the air, the accuser of the brethren, the old serpent, the great dragon, and the roaring lion.

Each name reveals something of the foul nature of the great adversary to the truth. In no uncertain terms, Satan is identified as a murderer, a liar, a sinner, a tempter, a perverter, a slanderer, a counterfeiter, and an oppressor. Martin Luther wrote of Satan, "His craft and power are great, and armed with cruel hate, on earth is not his equal."[1] He is, quite simply, "the evil one."

Satan's primary method of assault against the truth is to attack the veracity of God's Word. This ambush is a diabolical attempt to impugn the integrity of God's holy character. This attack on the truth reveals the devil's strategy, which remains unchanged since that fateful day. The war on the truth that began thousands of years ago in the garden of Eden continues to be carried out today against God Himself.

Casting Doubt upon the Truth

First, the devil began this combat by casting doubt upon the Word of God. A careful study of Genesis 3 reveals a clear progression in

1. Martin Luther, "A Mighty Fortress Is Our God" (c. 1529).

Satan's strategic attack against the truth in which the first attack was meant to create *doubt* in the mind of Eve. A master of deception, Satan launched his aggressive assault by planting his seeds of doubt in Eve's mind regarding the fidelity of God's Word. This plan of attack begins, "Now the serpent was more crafty than any other beast of the field that the LORD God had made" (Gen. 3:1). Satan, a fallen angel and spiritual being, possessed the body of a serpent, which became his mouthpiece.

Rightly does this passage state that the devil is "more crafty than any other beast in the field." Make no mistake, Satan is deceitful, conniving, scheming, calculating, crooked, tricky, and sneaky. With stealth and deception, he cornered Eve in the garden and initiated a frontal assault against her. In so doing, he unleashed his heavy artillery against the truth of God. In this camouflaged warfare, Satan spoke to Eve through the snake by uttering the first recorded question in the Bible. This is the question upon which the fate of humanity would turn: "Did God actually say . . . ?" (v. 1). The first words out of Satan's mouth were an attempt to lure Eve to question the veracity of the Word of God: "Has God really said this? Can you be sure? Is there some mistake in what He said?"

At the inception of his attack, Satan sought to cloud Eve's mind regarding the truthfulness of the Word of God. The serpent put his foot in the door of her mind in an attempt to pry it open and sow seeds of doubt. His goal was to destroy her trust in the truth. Where God had put a period, Satan sought to put a question mark. He cast aspersion upon the reliability of what God had declared. This hellish attack was masterful in its subtle deception.

Same Strategy, Same Satan

In the centuries that have since passed, Satan has not in the least altered his original strategy. He continues to make every attempt to cause people to doubt the Word of God. This is always the beginning point of his attack. Once he can pry open a person's mind and plant seeds of doubt, he will soon be able to cause that person to deny the Word altogether.

One present-day scene of a replicated ambush can be seen in the emerging church movement. This group regards any certainty one would have about the Word of God as a display of arrogance. They claim that uncertainty is a virtue to be lauded, a mark of true humility. One can almost hear the hiss of the serpent in the notion that uncertainty about the truth of God is a virtue to be praised, not a sin to be mortified. This ideology is a radical departure from the words spoken by Martin Luther: "Take away assertions and you take away Christianity."[2] Again, he said, "Christianity is a religion of assertions. All things that are in the Scripture are brought forth into the clearest light."[3] Luther is right. Christianity is marked by confident assertions that remove doubt in God's Word, far from what this movement touts.

Brian McLaren, one of the leaders of the emerging church has said, "Certainty can be dangerous."[4] He wrote elsewhere,

2. Martin Luther, *The Bondage of the Will*, ed. Jay P. Green (Lafayette, Ind.: Sovereign Grace, 2001), 11.

3. Ibid., 15.

4. "Brian McLaren Extended Interview," *Religion and Ethics NewsWeekly*, published July 15, 2005, accessed October 7, 2017, http://www.pbs.org

"I have gone out of my way to be unclear, reflecting my belief that clarity is overrated and that obscurity and intrigue often stimulate more thought than clarity."[5] The simplest way to summarize this leader's point of view would be to say darkness is preferred to light, lies are preferred to the truth, questions are better than convictions, and doubt is better than faith. This leader goes on to say, "If I seem to show too little respect for your opinions or thought, be assured, I have equal doubts about my own."[6] In other words, no one should be following this leader. By his own confession, he does not know where he is going.

Then he writes, "Orthodoxy is not a list of certain doctrines."[7] Do you hear the doubt being sprinkled into the minds of today's Christian readers? Let us be clear when we maintain that God has not stuttered or muttered in His Word. Neither has He edited His own truth. On the contrary, He has affirmed, "The grass withers, the flower fades, but the word of our God will stand forever" (Isa. 40:8). Yet this is the precise point at which Satan launches his attack. He tempts people to doubt the veracity of the Word of God.

/wnet/religionandethics/2005/07/15/july-15-2005-brian-mclaren-extended
-interview/11774/.

    5. Brian D. McLaren, *A Generous Orthodoxy* (Grand Rapids, Mich.: Zondervan, 2004), 23.

    6. Ibid., 19–20.

    7. Ibid., 293.

Distorting the Words of God

Second, Satan's attack, first aimed at producing doubt, is followed by the next strategy—distorting the words of God. The devil twisted what God had said by asking, "Did God actually say, 'You shall not eat of any tree in the garden'?" (Gen. 3:1). In asking this loaded question, Satan attributes to God words that He did not actually say. God had said, "You may surely eat of every tree of the garden" with the exception of the Tree of Knowledge of Good and Evil (2:16). Yet Satan shrewdly attributed to God the command, "You shall not eat of *any* tree in the garden." This was nearly the opposite of what God had actually said. Satan was cunning and deceptive as he sought to corrupt Eve's mind in regard to the truth of the Word of God.

Here, Satan essentially communicated to Eve, "I thought God loved you and was good, but He seems to be withholding His goodness from you. If He were truly good, He would provide for you. If God loved you, He would not be slapping your hand and keeping you from eating from the tree." The first woman was being drawn into dialogue with the devil, yet she had no idea of his true identity. Eve did not seem to be surprised at the notion of speaking with a serpent. Perhaps this indicates how early this temptation came. She received him as a credible messenger, perhaps thinking he was sent from heaven and was endowed with true understanding. What a sobering reminder this is that not all who claim to speak for God truly speak for Him. Instead, many who claim to speak for God actually speak for Satan. Unfortunately, many Christians have little discernment, just as Eve did not recognize the lie she was hearing.

As Eve relayed what God had spoken, she appeared to be already under the spell of the devil. Satan had misquoted God's words, and Eve went yet further away from God's words in her response. She replied, "We may eat of the fruit of the trees in the garden, but God said, 'You shall not eat of the fruit of the tree that is in the midst of the garden, neither shall you touch it, lest you die'" (Gen. 3:2–3). At this point, there appear three serious flaws in her handling of the Word of God.

First, she *took away* God's Word. God had said in Genesis 2:16, "You may surely eat of every tree of the garden," but Eve omitted the word *every*. She was playing fast and loose with the Word of God and had put one foot on a slippery slope with the devil. She minimized God's provision and discounted His goodness by omitting this one simple word. Second, Eve *added to* the Word of God by including the phrase "neither shall you touch it." God never prohibited Adam and Eve from touching any of the trees in the garden, but simply said of this one tree, "You shall not eat from it." In adding these words, Eve exaggerated God's strictness in His command. Third, Eve *softened* God's words. In Genesis 2:17, God had said, "You shall surely die." Downplaying the certainty of divine judgment, Eve dropped the word "surely." She simply said, "You shall not eat of the fruit . . . lest you die."

Revisionist Attacks Continue

Throughout the annals of human history, Eve's revisionist approach to God's Word has been emulated by countless others. Many have considered themselves to have liberty to omit portions of the Bible that they find unpalatable or lacking in cultural relevance. Others have added to the words of God in an attempt to encourage the modern-day reader to accept the Bible. But we must ask: Are we free to alter the Word of God? Is not the Word of God sufficient to bring about God's purposes on earth through its own intrinsic power? This deception, conceived in the garden of Eden, continues to thrive in our own day. Such tampering with the Word of God is nothing less than a frontal attack on the holiness of God, however innocuous it may appear to be.

This deception can be seen today in various modern translations of the Bible, as some scholars, editors, and publishing houses subtly alter the actual words of God. For example, the Bible translation called Today's New International Version removed the masculine pronouns for God in order to change how He has chosen to reveal Himself to man. Responding to these realities, John MacArthur said, "We live in a day when culture is telling the church what the Bible will be allowed to say. The TNIV has altered the Word of God to make it compatible with the contemporary, feminist, egalitarian movement."[8] MacArthur adds, "You do not take the Word of God, twist the Word of God, alter the Word of God, change the Word of God, embellish the Word of God, or diminish the Word of God in order to achieve something that accommodates cultural expectations."[9] This is

8. John MacArthur, "Assorted Attacks on the Bible," *Grace to You*, published August 27, 2006, accessed October 7, 2017, https://www.gty.org/library/sermons-library/90-320/assorted-attacks-on-the-bible.
9. Ibid.

however, exactly what is occurring with some Bible translations in our own day.

Hearing the Serpent's Hiss

Bible translators have one responsibility: to translate God's Word from the original Hebrew, Aramaic, and Greek as accurately as possible, allowing God to speak for Himself. They are not to change the Word in an attempt to appeal to the culture. They are simply the messengers of the Word of God, not the editors, and they must deliver it as entrusted to them. Many have departed from this commitment, seeking instead to spray cultural perfume on the Bible so that it might appeal to the current culture. The creator of another translation called the Voice says, "What we're trying to say is, we understand."[10] We ask ourselves, understand what? The Bible will always be unappealing to those who are dead in trespasses and sin. Does this give us license to alter the message to make it appealing to those in the flesh? The answer is a resounding no.

The aftermath of this dishonest endeavor is that "Thus says the Lord" can no longer be truly said. Instead, any translation that seeks to speak to modern sensibilities to accommodate its ignorance of biblical truth is guilty of distorting God's Word. As a case in point, the Voice's translation of John 1:1 reads, "Before

10. Fritz Lanham, "Scripture Gets a New Voice: New Testament Translation Presents Dialogue in Screenplay Format," *Houston Chronicle*, October 24, 2008, accessed October 7, 2017, http://www.chron.com/life/houston-belief/article/Scripture-gets-a-new-Voice-1764771.php.

time itself was measured, the Voice was speaking." There is significantly more involved in the Greek word *logos*—translated here as "voice"—in John 1:1 than simply, "the Voice was speaking." Here, the voice of God is minimized in the attempt to maximize customer satisfaction.

There are other translations that delete references to God's holy name. Others distort the relationship between God the Father and God the Son with alternate language, and delete references to submission to authority. The Word of God is being changed before our very eyes, despite the fact that God has spoken clearly on this issue. Deuteronomy 4:2 states, "You shall not add to the word that I command you, nor take from it." Proverbs 30:5–6 echoes, "Every word of God proves true. . . . Do not add to his words, lest he rebuke you and you be found a liar." Revelation 22:18 testifies, "I warn everyone who hears the words of the prophecy of this book: if anyone adds to them, God will add to him the plagues described in this book."

No man is free to alter the Word of God. Yet this is exactly what both Satan and Eve did in the garden. Unequivocally, we must take every precaution not to do the same.

Emphatically Denying the Truth

Third, Satan's next tactic is a brazen *denial* of the Word of God. He thrusts the sword yet deeper into the soul of Eve by telling her, "You will not surely die" (Gen. 3:4). The Father of Lies is so bent on perverting the truth that he attempts to characterize God as a liar. The devil now unloads all of the artillery of hell on Eve as he blatantly denies the integrity of the Word of God.

In the biblical languages, a word that was meant to be emphasized would be placed in the emphatic position, which is the front of the sentence. That is the case in Satan's response. Thus, the literal translation of this verse reads, "Not you will surely die." The emphasis is upon the word *not*. This is an all-out, no-holds-barred repudiation of the Word of God.

The first doctrine to come under attack by Satan is the truth of divine judgment. The truth found throughout Scripture is the promise of divine judgment upon man's sin: "The wages of sin is death" (Rom. 6:23), and "The soul who sins shall die" (Ezek. 18:20). But Satan told Eve the very opposite, that there would be no penalty for sin, much less death for disobedience. This blatant denial of divine judgment is still being propagated today. Rob Bell, a recent emerging church author whose books have skyrocketed to the very heights of the publishing world, wrote, "A staggering number of people have been taught that a select few Christians will spend forever in a peaceful, joyous place called heaven, while the rest of humanity spends forever in torment and punishment in hell with no chance for anything better."[11] He calls this view misguided, toxic, and subversive to the spread of Jesus' message.

In the process, Bell changes Jesus' message, turning it into a message that could be espoused by the Dalai Lama or Deepak Chopra. He says, "Millions and millions of people were taught

---

11. Rob Bell, *Love Wins: A Book About Heaven, Hell, and the Fate of Every Person Who Ever Lived* (New York: HarperCollins, 2011), viii.

that the center of the gospel is Jesus," as if to say, this idea is worthy of immediate rejection.[12] He claims that a good God bearing good news would never say He was going to send people to hell unless they believe upon the name of Jesus Christ.

The Necessity of Preaching Judgment

However, the message of divine judgment is an essential part of God's truth. God's judgment on sin is a necessary expression of His holiness. Divine wrath serves as the black velvet backdrop that causes the diamond of God's grace to shine brighter than the sun. If the black velvet backdrop of God's divine wrath and the reality of eternity in hell were removed, the good news of salvation would evoke no more response from sinners than a mere yawn. Bell goes on to write, "The most powerful things happen when the church surrenders its desire to convert people. The church must stop thinking about everybody primarily in categories of in or out, saved or not, believer or unbeliever. This is offensive."[13] To be sure, this is a full assault on the truth and a severe departure from what the Word of God says.

This modern-day deceiver also says, "Sometimes people use Jesus' name, other times they don't. Some people have so much baggage with regard to the name Jesus that when they encounter it, the last thing they're inclined to name is Jesus. When you share the message, just take out the name Jesus, because people

12. Ibid.
13. Rob Bell, *Velvet Elvis: Repainting the Christian Faith* (Grand Rapids, Mich.: Zondervan, 2009), 167.

have a lot of hang-ups with that name, and just use any name other than the name for Jesus."[14] This is the polar opposite of what Peter said: "There is salvation in no one else, for there is no other name under heaven given among men by which we must be saved" (Acts 4:12). The Bible states, "For there is one God, and there is one mediator between God and men, the man Christ Jesus, who gave himself as a ransom for all, which is the testimony given at the proper time" (1 Tim. 2:5–6).

Bell continues, "If your God is loving one second and cruel the next, if your God will punish people for all eternity for sins committed in just a few years, no amount of clever marketing or compelling language, or good music, or great coffee will be able to disguise that one glaring, unacceptable, awful reality, which is that God meant what He said, 'Now in the day you eat of this fruit, you will surely die.'"[15] How subtle are the lies of Satan.

Liberalism's Lethal Lies

This outright denial of the Word of God has been occurring in liberal seminaries and among liberal theologians for decades. Opponents claim that the biblical writers were simply writing out of their own insight and were no more inspired than Shakespeare with his plays. However, smart men do not write books that condemn themselves, as the Bible authors did, and smart men do not say that they cannot save themselves. The attack of partial inspiration argues that some parts of the Bible are more

14. Bell, *Love Wins*, 153.
15. Ibid., 175.

inspired than other parts. In other words, Jesus was inspired, but Paul was not. However, Paul and all the other writers of Scripture claimed that they wrote under the direct influence of the Holy Spirit of God.

The idea of concept inspiration is an attack on Scripture that states that only the ideas, not the words, of the Bible are inspired. However, Jesus clearly stated, "Man shall not live by bread alone, but by every word that comes from the mouth of God" (Matt. 4:4). The fact is, we cannot have concepts without words any more than we can have mathematics without numbers, music without notes, or art without color.

The idea of existential inspiration is another attack that says that the only parts of the Bible that are inspired are the ones that personally speak to the individual. Others lines of attack claim that there are fallacies throughout Scripture. We must understand that these attacks are as old as the garden. They follow in the footsteps of the first temptation that came slithering onto the page of redemptive history. These outright and blatant attacks on the truth of God in His Word continue in our day.

Assassinating God's Character

Fourth, Satan escalates his attack from a denial of God's Word to an outright *defamation* of God Himself. He whispered to Eve, "For God knows that when you eat of it your eyes will be opened" (Gen. 3:5). This was a deliberate attempt to place God in a bad light by insinuating that His threat of death was nothing more than a scare tactic to keep Adam and Eve in their place. God was obviously selfish and jealous that they might know too much and ascend to His heights. This was a slander of God's holy character. It was an outright denunciation of His goodness, an assertion that God desired to prevent Eve from enjoying the goodness of His creation. The attack was meant to denigrate the mercy of God by maintaining that He is keeping all good things to Himself. With a narcissistic self-egoism, Satan implied that God was enjoying keeping Eve from the pleasures that He desired to hoard for Himself.

This sinister attack of Satan against the truth continues even to this day on many fronts. The lie is still being spread in the minds of many that following the Word of God will mean that He will withhold pleasures from those who follow its teaching. But this is a lie of the devil, and it must be recognized as such.

Deifying Man's Status

This fateful dialogue in the garden descended yet lower, finally, to the *deification of the creature*. Whenever God is brought down, man is raised up. Satan sought to clench Eve's disobedience with a final knockout punch by saying, "And you will be like God, knowing good and evil" (Gen. 3:5). This was the promise that she would become like God. By taking the fruit, Eve was promised that she would become the equal of God. This meant that she would be able to decide for herself between right and wrong. This way, she would have no need

97

for divine truth. She could make up her own rules and draw her own line in the sand. She could run her life exactly as she desired. She would not need the Word of God, for she would be able to say, "I know what is right for me." Supposedly, she would be able to see what God sees and know what He knows. This was not a temptation to fall down but rather a seductive lure to fall up. The seduction was not to be like the devil but to be like God.

Most people would deny that they would ever fall for such a temptation as this. Who in their right mind would actively seek to deify themselves over God? Yet mankind has been attempting to do this since that fatal day in the garden. For example, the Mormons teach that as man now is, God once was, and as God now is, man may be. This is nothing more and nothing less than this same lie of Satan regarding the deification of man. In addition, Paul Crouch, the founder of Trinity Broadcasting Network said, "I am a little God. I have His name. I am one with Him. I am in covenant relation. I am a little God."[16] Such audacious blasphemy is frightening.

One notorious leader of the Word of Faith movement said, "You don't have a god in you; you are one."[17] This idolatry is also espoused by the New Age movement. Even worse, the Roman Catholic Church states in its catechism, "'For the Son of God became man so that we might become God.' 'The only-begotten son of God, wanting to make us share in his divinity, assumed

---

16. *Praise the Lord*, July 7, 1986.
17. Kenneth Copeland, *The Force of Love* (Fort Worth, Tex.: Kenneth Copeland Ministries, 1987), audiotape 02-0028, side 1.

our nature so that as he, made man, might make men gods.'"[18] How deceptive are the lies of Satan, and how gullible mankind can be.

Dying without the Truth

What is the result of yielding to the devil's lies in this war on the Word? This broad path leads to only one destination: death. The Bible states, "So when the woman saw that the tree was good for food, and that it was a delight to the eyes, and that the tree was to be desired to make one wise, she took of its fruit and ate, and she also gave some to her husband who was with her, and he ate" (Gen. 3:6). Elsewhere, the Scripture clearly teaches that the sin of one man became the sin of the entire world (Rom. 5:12). Death entered the world through the sin of this one man, Adam, and the entire human race became guilty of this one act of disobedience to the Word of God. Disobedience always leads to death—physically, emotionally, spiritually, and eternally.

Further, the departure from God's Word also leads to the death of any Christian ministry, institution, seminary, denomination, or missions organization. The graveyards of history are filled with seminaries and denominations that fall away from the truth. Such a departure also causes the death of true preaching. Moreover, apostasy leads to the death of soul-winning efforts in evangelism, of personal holiness, and

18. Catechism of the Catholic Church, 1.2.2.3.1.1.

of godliness. Simply put, any departure from the Scripture is a departure from God Himself. No individual or group can long survive this.

This is the war on the Word, and the consequences and ramifications of this war are eternal. R. Albert Mohler, president of The Southern Baptist Theological Seminary, has correctly written, "The most contentious debates among Christians are at their most fundamental level arguments over biblical inerrancy and authority. The issues of greatest debate in our time fall along the fault line of biblical inerrancy and authority."[19] Mohler is right that human history is nothing more than a battle for the truthfulness of truth. The same can be said of church history. The accuracy and authority of Scripture have existed at the heart of most major Christian controversies. The frontline battle in the church will always be over the inspiration, inerrancy, and authority of Scripture.

The Bible is a lamp unto the feet and a light unto the path. It is life-giving seed sown in the heart that brings forth eternal life. The Word of God is nourishing milk for the soul, sweeter than honey, and more precious than gold. It is a hammer that breaks the rock into pieces and a sharp two-edged sword that pierces to the division of soul and spirit. The Word of Truth is water that washes, cleanses, and renews, and apart from this Book, there is no salvation and no sanctification.

---

19. Albert Mohler, "Biblical Authority: Must We Accept the Words of Scripture?" *Albert Mohler*, March 22, 2006, accessed October 7, 2017, http://www.albertmohler.com/2006/03/22/biblical-authority-must-we-accept-the-words-of-scripture.

In our moment in human history, we must advance and hold the battle line secure for the next generation. We must be fully engaged as this war on the Word rages, seeking to uphold the standard of sound words and earnestly contend for the faith. May God give us, His people, renewed confidence in the authority and infallibility of this pure and perfect Book, the written Word of God.

6

TRUTH UNDER ASSAULT

The Rejection of Truth by an Unbelieving Age

Pilate's age-old question "What is truth?" was laced with deadly cynicism and contempt, and it continues to poison the minds of many. We live in a world riddled with unbelief, a world in which a new enemy of the truth has emerged known as the New Atheism. With an unholy defiance, these unbelieving forces are being raised up by Satan to boldly resist the truth as never before. This atheistic agenda is hell-bent on the complete destruction of the truth of God. The New Atheism is aggressively militant, as it launches a frontal assault against every form of Christian truth.

Writing in *Letters to a Young Contrarian*, the renowned atheist Christopher Hitchens asserted, "I am not even an atheist so much as I am an antitheist."[1] In other words, he not only

---

1. Christopher Hitchens, *Letters to a Young Contrarian* (New York: Basic, 2009), 55.

believed that there is no God, but he was adamantly opposed to even the thought of God. He was more than a God-denier, but a God-hater. Consequently, he did everything in his power to oppose anyone's belief in the existence of God. Hitchens added, "I not only maintain that all religions are versions of the same untruth, but I hold that the influence of churches and the effect of religious belief is positively harmful."[2] With these statements, Hitchens adamantly opposed any notion of the absolute truth from God.

Out of the Closet

In his best-selling book *The God Delusion*, another well-known atheist, Oxford professor Richard Dawkins, brazenly espoused his zeal for atheism. He wrote, "I am quite keen on the politics of persuading people of the virtues of atheism."[3] He went on to estimate the number of nonreligious people in the United States as somewhere around thirty million people. Dawkins wrote, "I think we're in the same position as the gay movement was a few decades ago. There was a need then for people to come out. The more people who came out, the more people have had courage."[4] In citing this recent social precedence with the homosexual agenda, he called upon atheists to come out of their closets, march down Main Street, and raise their voices.

---

2. Ibid.

3. Gary Wolf, "The Church of the Non-Believers," *Wired*, November 1, 2006, accessed October 7, 2017, https://www.wired.com/2006/11/atheism.

4. Ibid.

He noted, "They are more numerous than anybody realizes."[5] Undoubtedly, militant atheism is on the rise today.

With evangelistic zeal, Dawkins intends to bring down God's design for the family and capture our children for atheism. He writes, "How much do we regard children as being the property of their parents?"[6] The radical agenda he seeks to spread is this: parents should not be allowed to "brainwash" their children into believing in God. Parents should not be free to impose their beliefs on their children.[7] Apparently, atheists should be allowed this access to our children. According to this hell-bent agenda, children should be taught there is no God and, consequently, no absolute truth of God.

Dawkins argues that it is morally wrong to foist bad ideas upon children. In other words, it is morally wrong for you to read Bible stories to your children at night. It is morally wrong for you to take your children to church. It is morally wrong for you to raise up your children in the fear and admonition of the Lord. He goes on to say such indoctrination is the ultimate child abuse. This is the gathering storm that is swirling in our godless culture.

The New Evangelists

Gary Wolf, a contributing editor at *Wired* magazine, writes, "The new atheists condemn not just belief in God, but they condemn

---

5. Ibid.
6. Ibid.
7. See Richard Dawkins, *The God Delusion* (New York: Houghton Mifflin Harcourt, 2008), 18, 25, 367–80.

respect for belief in God. Religion is not only wrong; it is evil."[8] Wolf sees Dawkins as a persuasive evangelist for atheism. He writes, "Evangelism is a moral imperative for the atheist. Dawkins does not merely disagree with religious myths; he disagrees with tolerating them."[9] It is not enough that the new atheists choose to reject the truth of God. They are zealous that everyone else does as well.

This is the world of unbelief in which we find ourselves. This is, in part, the spirit of the age that is pressing in around us. The question is, in the face of this new atheism, how are Christians to stand firm? What is our response to such outright attacks on God and the Christian faith? How do we live in a culture that rejects the truth? The answers to these questions begin with a careful examination of the truth of the Scripture itself.

The key passage that we will investigate in this chapter is Psalm 14, which is a psalm of David. It was written at a difficult time when the psalmist found himself surrounded by godless nations that mocked the existence of the true God. So, David addressed these atheists in his day with words that are helpful for us to hear in our day. There is nothing new under the sun. The atheists whom David addressed are the same as in our day.

The Denial of God

David begins this psalm by addressing the atheists in his time. "The fool says in his heart, 'There is no God'" (Ps. 14:1). The word "fool" in Hebrew does not mean a person of mental incompetence,

---

8. Wolf, "The Church of the Non-Believers."
9. Ibid.

but one of moral perversity. He is not a fool in the sense that he lacks the intellectual capacity to rightly connect his thoughts and draw proper conclusions. Such people are often some of the world's most highly intelligent people with impeccable academic credentials. This text asserts that fools do not have a head problem but a heart problem. The fool is one who spurns the clear evidence concerning the existence of God. He chooses to make a fundamental decision to reject God in his unbelief despite the convincing proof before him. He makes a deliberate rejection and intentional refusal of God Himself. To say that there is no God makes one a fool.

As previously indicated, this rejection of God takes place in the heart: "The fool says in his heart." The heart refers to the entire inner person, encompassing much more than simply the emotions. To the ancient Hebrew, the heart represented a person's entire inner life. It was inclusive of one's mind, emotions, conscience, and will. The atheist has made this deliberate denial of God in his heart. It is important to note that in the Hebrew, the words "there is" are not found in the original manuscripts. The Bible translators have supplied this subject and verb to make the statement read more smoothly. But in the original language, this denial simply reads, "The fool has said in his heart, no God."

In other words, the atheist knows that God exists, but intentionally refuses Him. In the depths of his soul, the fool has said, "No God." In other words, "There is no God for me. I will have nothing to do with God." This fool refuses to acknowledge God in his life. He will not let God run his life or tell him how to live. He will be the captain of his own ship, the master of his own soul.

When the truth of God is presented to him through creation and conscience, and even special revelation, the atheist rigidly bows his back, stiffens his neck, and sets his jaw. He says, "No God."

There are different types of atheists. The *intellectual* atheist claims from the standpoint of science or reason that there is no God. However, in his heart, he knows that God exists. The *religious* atheist has repudiated the one true living God as clearly presented in the Scripture. He chooses instead to go after gods of his own making. The *practical* atheist believes that there is a God, but chooses to live his life independent of God, thus rejecting God. Regardless of the type, all atheists have rejected God and have reduced themselves to fools.

Denouncing the Truth

The Apostle Paul addresses the atheist in the first chapter of Romans. The truth about God, he writes, is clearly made known to all men in the creation all around them. They are without excuse before God, Paul argues. Yet they intentionally suppress, refuse, and reject this revealed truth. They instead choose to live in unrighteousness without God in their life. According to verse 19, there is a knowledge of God—a "God-consciousness"—placed within every man and woman. The truth about God is evident within them, because God has made it evident to them through general revelation. This self-disclosure of God is presented to all people and includes the knowledge of the existence of God.

But this general revelation is not sufficient to know God in a saving relationship. To truly know God requires special revelation, which is found in the gospel truth of His written Word. While general revelation is not enough to save man, it is sufficient to hold him accountable to God for his suppression and rejection of truth. Every person, therefore, is without excuse before God.

Disregarding the Creator

This general revelation of the existence of God is seen through creation: "For his invisible attributes, namely, his eternal power and divine nature, have been clearly perceived, ever since the creation of the world, in the things that have been made" (Rom. 1:20). God's attributes are clearly displayed in the universe He has made. The mere fact that there is creation necessitates an adequate cause. There is only one reasonable, rational explanation for the creation of the universe, and it is the existence of a Creator. Everyone should know that out of nothing, nothing comes. There is no impersonal force or random explosion in outer space that could have created everything out of nothing, much less with the perfect design it all possesses.

Any thinking person can look at creation and see something about God—who He is and what He is like. Creation itself reveals that God is a transcendent Creator who is immense and powerful. He has created the world with order and balance with genius design. The changing of the four seasons, the spinning of the earth on its axis, the maintaining of the earth's precisely proper angle, and the placement of the earth at the perfect distance from the sun in order to sustain life clearly testify that there is a God of unimaginable genius. Moreover, the Creator has made mankind with extraordinary brilliance of design in His own image. God has revealed Himself outwardly through creation and internally through the conscience, embedding in the human soul the essential truth that He exists. God is not silent but speaks through divine revelation. This God has made Himself known to us so that the atheist is without excuse.

Yet despite this knowledge of God, men do not honor Him as God. The human race has made an intentional choice to withhold the honor, praise, and glory that should be given to this all-powerful, all-glorious Creator. Men stubbornly choose not to honor Him as God or give Him thanks. They choose to reject the revelation of God, and this puts them on a downward spiral that will ultimately cast them down to the fires of hell. These God-rejecters, Paul writes, become futile in their speculations. As they turn away from the light of truth, they step into the darkness of lies about the meaning and purpose of life. As a result, their foolish hearts are darkened.

The Mind Darkened

When people intentionally resist the light of the truth concerning the existence of God, it results in their being given over to the darkness of idolatrous thoughts and unbelief toward God. If men choose to resist the truth about God, they commit spiritual suicide. Paul says of such people that "claiming to be wise, they became fools" (Rom. 1:22). *Foolish* does not mean that they have lost their intellect. They still teach in the university and write books. These academic giants still possess towering intellects and soaring IQs. However, they can no longer see the truth because they are so hardened in their foolish unbelief.

They "exchanged the glory of the immortal God"—meaning the knowledge about God—and discarded it for man-made "images" (Rom. 1:23). These are idols made in man's own likeness, whether with their hands or in their minds. Thus, the atheist worships what his own mind can conjure about what God is like rather than bowing before the true God. In reality, the atheist is worshiping himself. To be sure, atheism is a religion, the final step in the downward spiral of rejecting God. Atheism involves rejecting the true knowledge of God and replacing it with the false worship of self.

The Insanity of Atheism

The insanity of atheism claims that nothing times no one equals everything. They believe that everything came out of nothing. They adhere to the view that the design, order, and beauty that we see in the world just happened by chance. The only god left for the atheist to worship is himself.

What Paul teaches in Romans 1 is the same thing that David affirms in Psalm 14. This is the atheist's denial, that when the truth about God is made known to him, he is not saying that there is no God. Rather, his spiritual problem runs much deeper. The atheist, in reality, is saying no to God. He does not want God in his life. Neither does he want His truth to rule and reign over him. When he says there is no God, he desires autonomy.

Humanist John Dewey, coauthor of the *Humanist Manifesto I* in 1933, declared, "There is no God, and there is no soul. Hence, there are no needs for the props of traditional religion. With dogma and creed excluded, then immutable truth is also dead and buried. There is no room for fixed, natural law or moral absolutes."[10] Here is the real reason the atheist wants to escape the face of the existence of God. Dewey says it plainly. It is so that there is no "immutable truth" with which he is confronted and held accountable. The atheist rejects God so he can live his life however he desires.

The Corruption Within

The atheist's denial is deeply rooted in the atheist's depravity. The psalmist writes, "They are corrupt" (Ps. 14:1). The word translated "corrupt" means "rotten" or "ruined," and it was used to describe milk that had soured. That is to say, their character is rotten on the inside. David contends, "They have committed abominable deeds." This is true of every person in this world who is outside of saving faith in Jesus Christ—the human race is utterly depraved. Those who reject God commit abominable deeds of irreverence and blasphemy. There is no restraint of their tongues as they speak out against the God of heaven and shake their puny fists in His face.

The psalmist goes on to say, "There is none who does good" (v. 1). That is a universal condemnation referring to everyone outside of Christ, but specifically in this context, it refers to the

---

10. Cited in William Nitardy, *Understanding the Anatomy of Evil* (Denver: Outskirts, 2016), 108.

atheist who rejects God. Here is God's assessment of the atheist: he is not merely mistaken but malevolent. This is so fundamental to the fallen nature of man that Paul quotes this verse in Romans 3:10–12 as he makes God's indictment of the entire human race.

The Death of Reason

David continues, "The LORD looks down from heaven on the children of man, to see if there are any who understand, who seek after God" (Ps. 14:2). As God looks down from heaven, by human analogy, He must squint to see the small, minuscule stature of feeble man who says there is no God. He strains to look down as though He has to search for this insignificant little person who is standing up and declaring his rejection of God. As it were, God must peer to see if any understand the insanity of their rejection when they have the knowledge of His existence made evident within them.

The psalmist asks "if there are any who understand" (v. 2). The conclusion is negative. There are none who understand their need to submit to God. This is why there are none "who seek after God" (v. 2). They are enslaved by a mind that does not understand. Thus, they have a will that does not choose to seek after God. They are blind leaders of the blind, living in the darkness of the dark. They are not seeking God, but rather running away from Him as fast as they can.

The conclusion is, "They have all turned aside; together they have become corrupt; there is none who does good, not even one" (v. 3). They have each one turned away from God to go their own way. For the second time, David says they are "corrupt"—a double reinforcement. Not a single one of them does good in the eyes of God. Everything they do is tainted with sin.

God has weighed the atheist in the balance and found him utterly wanting. Those who reject the truth of God are intellectual lightweights, no matter how smart they are. They have fallen woefully short of the glory of God. But they are no different from anyone else who languishes in unbelief. All have fallen short of the glory of God. This is what God sees as He looks down from heaven and scrutinizes the atheist.

Detesting the Believers

David asks a rhetorical question: "Have they no knowledge, all the evildoers who eat up my people as they eat bread and do not call upon the LORD?" (Ps. 14:4). The answer is no. They do not have knowledge. They do not know that the Lord sees them. They do not know that they are storing up wrath until the day of wrath. They have tried to eradicate God from their minds. In so doing, they have become ignorant of the most basic truth.

Instead, David says, they "eat up my people as they eat bread." Because they hate the truth of God, they therefore hate the people of God. This is the only logical consistency about them. They want to grind up believers with their teeth like a ravenous animal, devour them as captured prey, and remove them from the world. In brazen defiance, they attack believers in an attempt to be rid of God. They attempt to remove all people who mention the name of God in order to have nothing to do with God. They cannot even bear to hear the name of God.

Does not the atheist know that the day is coming when he will stand before God? Is he entirely ignorant of this day that is looming on the horizon of eternity? The day is fast approaching when the atheist will be directly confronted with the reality of God. In that day, the true existence and holy nature of God will be made fully known to him as he comes to stand before the divine tribunal and must give an account for his rejection of the truth.

Despising the Poor

David then turns to address the foolish atheist directly: "You would shame the plans of the poor" (Ps. 14:6). The "poor" refers to the believers whom they had sought to intimidate, badger, and persecute. These believers were afflicted because the atheist had risen up and sought to bring much perversity and difficulty and affliction upon them.

The atheist desires to shame not simply believers but ultimately the name of God. He hates the very thought of God, and he seeks to put to shame not merely the messenger, but God Himself. The atheist rises up in unholy hatred against the God whom we love and serve.

So depraved is the fool who rejects God that he preys upon the most vulnerable in society, the poor. He tries to thwart what few plans the poor have to advance in this world. The atheist is so self-consumed that he even takes advantage of those without any financial possessions. But be assured, not only does David see this, but God sees it and will remember it in the final judgment.

Concerning the poor who has trust in God, David says "the LORD is his refuge" (v. 6). Though these atheistic evildoers assail the poor, God Himself will protect them. If not in this world, God will certainly be their refuge in the coming judgment and in the world to come. Those without anything in this world, nevertheless, have everything in God. Those who put their trust in God find Him to be their refuge, a stronghold in the day of trouble. Though the atheist attempts to devour the poor believers, God will have the final word. The Lord will be their protection and deliver them from the judgment that will be unleashed upon the wicked.

Let us remember that God is our unassailable refuge in the midst of this present storm. God is our stronghold and our fortress. It matters not how the atheist rages against God and seeks to throw off all divine authority. We can withstand any gathering storm that is bringing opposition against our faith. In fact, the greater the storm, the deeper the roots of the tree grow. So it is with our faith in God. No one can take God down. Therefore, we are secure. When God is our refuge, we are immovable. God is the impregnable citadel of all who call upon His name and put their trust in Him. The contrast could not be any greater between the fool who has said in his heart that there is no God, who will stand in dread on that final day, and believers, who have put their faith and trust in the Lord Jesus Christ and will stand unafraid in the day of judgment.

Let us take confidence as the tumultuous tempest of atheism swirls around us. As atheists come stepping out of the shadows seeking to intimidate, let us be reminded that they are but fools who have built upon the sand. There is coming a final storm in the last day, the day of God's wrath—a day of great dread for them. All who refuse the revelation of God and refuse to build upon the rock of truth, choosing instead to build upon the sand, will fall greatly.

Dreading in the End

When the final day appears, the atheist will be in total dread. They will be in shock as they stand before the God whom they have rejected. Psalm 14:5 reads, "There they are in great terror, for God is with the generation of the righteous." As David sees the final outcome of the atheist, he sees them on the last day in the judgment. He notes that they will be in shock when they stand before God. The Creator will be their Judge, and they will have nowhere to hide and no excuse to offer.

The atheist will discover that "God is with the generation of the righteous." God stands with those whom He has declared to be righteous and who live righteous lives. Conversely, God does not stand with the atheist but opposes him with the full fury of His holy wrath.

The atheists of the world are resolute in their hatred of God, but a time is coming at the end of the age when they will be filled with great dread. Great terror, panic, and alarm will seize them. Eyes will bulge, hearts will melt, knees will buckle, legs will shake, and palms will sweat. It will be the worst nightmare that has ever come upon them. It will be a day of dread in that final day, as the just judgment of God will come.

David concludes, "Oh, that salvation for Israel would come out of Zion! When the LORD restores the fortunes of his people, let Jacob rejoice, let Israel be glad" (v. 7). In other words, David longs for God's deliverance of His people from evildoers who attack the righteous. He longs for the time when the Lord will establish His kingdom upon the earth. In anticipation of that final day, God's people should rejoice and be glad because He will ultimately establish His righteous rule from the heavenly Zion.

Dying in Unbelief

When the atheist dies, he will have no place or refuge in God. He has no imputed righteousness from the Lord. He has no knowledge of God. He has no salvation out of the heavenly Zion. He has no fortunes in God. He has nothing—no grace, no rejoicing, no gladness.

Christopher Hitchens, the atheist mentioned above, died December 15, 2011. His last words were to believers, strangely, as he asked them not to pray for him. Then he warned against any claims that would be made, that on his deathbed he might change his mind. He said that if anyone heard anything from his lips other than total defiance of God, they were to assume that he was under the influence of drugs or that he had lost his mental faculties.[11] He was adamant in his refusal to call upon the Lord until the end. This defiance has now surely turned to dread.

Let us give thanks that we have been rescued from playing the fool, who has said there is no God. Let us be humble with contrite spirits, remembering that divine grace, not our own goodness, has taught us that there is a God in heaven, who is Lord of heaven and earth. The day is fast approaching when every knee will bow and every tongue will confess that Jesus Christ is Lord to the glory of God the Father. The rejection of the truth will lead to eternal ruin for all who deny the existence and lordship of Jesus Christ. As we stand with boldness in a culture that rejects the truth, may we courageously and persistently hold fast to and hold forth the Word of Truth.

11. Nick Cohen, "Deathbed Conversion? Never. Christopher Hitchens was Defiant to the Last," *The Guardian*, June 4, 2016, accessed October 9, 2017, https://www.theguardian.com/commentisfree/2016/jun/04/deathbed-conversion-christopher-hitchens-defiant-to-last.

7

COMPROMISING THE TRUTH

The Rejection of Truth by a Worldly Church

As we survey the world scene, we can easily detect the rejection of the absolute truth of God in every realm of society. Anyone with spiritual eyes has no difficulty identifying this outright refusal. Given the total depravity of the human heart, this resistance is to be expected. But what surprises us, and even astonishes us, is when we see this same rejection of truth in a realm where we would least expect it. I refer to the rejection of truth within the very walls of the church. Sadly, the church in this hour has often become a place where the truth of God is under its greatest attack.

As the moon comes between the sun and the earth, causing an eclipse and leaving the planet in darkness, we are witnessing in these days the obstruction of the truth of God in vastly larger ways. This veiling of the Word of God is occurring in the church to an alarming extent. The brilliant splendor of the truth of

Scripture is being concealed in the church today by humanistic wisdom and worldly entertainment. Tragically, this blockage is occurring in the very place where the truth ought to shine the brightest.

In this present hour, the message of the Scripture is being shrouded and withheld from the people in the pews. Whenever this occurs, *Ichabod* is written over the front door of the church—"the glory of the Lord has departed." If the church is to recover her mission in the world, the truth of God must be front and center again, and she must return to being the lamp-stand she was intended by God to be. If the church is to walk in the light and reflect the glory of God, she must reclaim the truth in every area.

I want us to consider some critically important areas in which we see the truth being compromised and concealed in the church. It is said that a right diagnosis is half the cure. That being so, here are five critical areas where the diagnosis reveals that the truth of God is being obscured in the church—in her pulpit, theology, worship, methodology, and evangelism.

Concealed in Preaching

First and foremost, the truth is being concealed in many pulpits today. The light of truth is revealed in the pages of Scripture, which is a light to our path and a lamp to our feet (Ps. 119:105). When the Word of Truth is preached, the blazing light of the truth shines brightly. However, when the preacher departs from the Bible, the truth is hidden and its light is concealed. In such cases, a spiritual darkness covers the land. The pulpit immediately loses both its power and authority. This is, tragically, the case in many churches.

In many pulpits, the truth is shrouded by human eloquence, personal experiences, and situational ethics. These have replaced "Thus says the Lord." In many houses of worship, social causes, cultural progress, and countless other subjects have captured the focus of preaching. While some of these matters may find a proper place in the church, the sad reality is that they have replaced the primacy of straightforward biblical preaching. Where the exposition of Scripture and the authoritative declaration are abandoned, the message of salvation is darkened and the church becomes a glorified social club.

One noted observer of the evangelical scene, Bible scholar Merrill Unger, wrote years ago, "To an alarming extent, the glory is departing from the pulpit of the twentieth century. The basic reason for this gloomy condition is obvious. That which imparts the glory has been taken away from the center of so much of our modern preaching, and placed on the periphery."[1] This is to say, the truth of God has been denied the throne and given a subordinate glory.

Famine in the Land

The prophet Amos warned of such days when the Word of God would be withheld from preaching: "'Behold, the days are

1. Merrill F. Unger, "The Need of Expository Preaching in the Twentieth Century," *Bibliotheca Sacra* 111 (July–September 1954): 231.

coming,' declares the Lord GOD, 'when I will send a famine on the land—not a famine of bread, nor a thirst for water, but of hearing the words of the LORD'" (Amos 8:11). Such a severe shortage of spiritual bread results in emaciated faith and a shriveled confidence in God. The people faint from the lack of nourishment for their famished souls. God goes on to warn, "They shall wander from sea to sea, and from north to east; they shall run to and fro, to seek the word of the LORD, but they shall not find it" (v. 12). In other words, no matter where they look, the truth cannot be found.

We are living in such days of drought. Walk into the average church and you will most likely not be served an adult portion of the truth. Instead, a steady diet of spiritual junk food is being given. The Word has been withheld, and a new way of doing church has emerged. Exposition is now being exchanged for entertainment, and preaching is supplanted by performances. Doctrine is being replaced by drama and theology with theatrics. The pulpit, once the focal point of the church, is being overshadowed by trendy worship extravaganzas and pageantry. In this tragic exchange, the truth of God is being withheld from spiritually starving people.

Solomon addressed such desperate days: "Where there is no prophetic vision the people cast off restraint, but blessed is he who keeps the law" (Prov. 29:18). The word "vision" refers to the divine revelation that came through the prophets and was to be given to the people. In the parallelism of this verse, it was also used synonymously with "the law." Where there is no prophetic vision as revealed in the law of God, there is no revelation from

God being given to the people. Where there is an absence of truth, there is an absence of true godly living.

The reason for this famine in the land lies not only with the pulpit but with the people. God sends His preachers to proclaim the Word. They are God's gifts to His people (Eph. 4:8–11). But if the people refuse to hear and heed the word spoken by His servants, the time may come when God will no longer send His preachers in abundance. The cause for the famine lies with the hard-heartedness of the people. If what has been given is not received by faith, then even what they have will be taken away. To whom much is given, much will be required.

The Apostle Paul warned of such times when churches would no longer desire Bible preaching: "For the time is coming when people will not endure sound teaching, but having itching ears they will accumulate for themselves teachers to suit their own passions, and will turn away from listening to the truth and wander off into myths" (2 Tim. 4:3–4). This refers to churches that do not want a Bible preacher who will declare the truth of God. These pulpit search committees are no longer looking for expository preachers. Instead, they are looking for the man who will tickle their ears and massage their egos. Many churches today are looking for a CEO or church growth expert for a pastor and have no desire for a biblical expositor. There is an eclipse of the truth of God in the pulpit of the evangelical church.

Surely, we are living in days in which there is an alarming scarcity of the unvarnished truth in pulpits and little desire for it by the people. One reason many people have no appetite for biblical preaching is because they have so rarely, if ever, heard it. The dearth of biblical preaching has caused an eclipse of the glory of God in the evangelical church today. Whenever this rejection of truth occurs, these churches are cloaked in darkness.

Compromised in Theology

Second, we also see the compromise of the truth in the area of theology. The study of biblical theology reveals the vital truth about God Himself. It is the teaching of sound doctrine that displays His awesome glory in vivid array. But if the truth of God is veiled, churches will be malnourished. Such a theological compromise is now occurring as congregations are being fed a steady diet of how-to, applicational sermons. We have lost the true knowledge of who God is, as the teaching of the church is becoming more and more about man and less and less about God. Pulpits have become more about the culture and less about Christ, more about tolerance and less about truth.

Historically, the highest points in the church have always been when the church has had the highest view of God. High theology produces high worship and holy living. But low views of God lead to low worship and gutter living. No church will rise any higher than its thoughts of God.

When the church departs from Reformed theology, she inevitably begins a descent downward into the weakened state of Arminianism and antinomianism. But this fall from truth rarely stops there. This slippery slope causes the descent to pick up speed toward liberalism that rejects the absolute authority of the Scripture. The descent then spirals down to ecumenism, which views all religions as possessing some part of the truth. This teaches that many roads lead to God, and Christianity is simply one of those paths. Ecumenism then cascades down yet further with greater rapidity to universalism, which is the erroneous belief that all men will be saved in the end. Some even go so far as to say that the devil himself will be saved in the end.

From universalism, the descent plunges yet deeper into agnosticism, which is the belief that no one can be certain what the truth is. Uncertainty is hailed as a virtue. Humility is defined as accepting that no one can know the truth. Agnosticism claims that since no one can really know the truth about God, we need to hold our doubts in an open hand and share our uncertainty with one another. Finally, this descent reaches rock bottom as this slippery slope crashes into the eternal flames of atheism. The rejection of the existence of God is the deepest abyss in which the fool says in his heart there is no God (Ps. 14:1).

In our own time, we are seeing this very eclipse of the truth in the theology of the church. We see it being usurped in open theism, the false teaching that attempts to blindfold God lest He see the future. We see the truth veiled in charismatic teachings that claim that new, extrabiblical revelation is still being given by God to the church. We see it in Arminianism, which seeks to bind the sovereignty of God in salvation and diminish the effects of the fall. We see it in the false gospel of baptismal regeneration, the heretical teaching that one must be baptized in order to be saved. We see the truth concealed in the Free Grace movement, which attempts to deny the right of the Lord Jesus Christ to rule over the life of the believer. Many other areas of theology are under attack today, putting the evangelical church on the slippery slope toward a powerless state.

Only God knows where we are on this slippery slope. Our task is to recover the high ground of a God-centered theology. We must fight the good fight for the truth and, if need be, take the path of greatest resistance. We must scale this mountain of high truth and replant the banner of the sovereign grace of our God. The withholding of truth in the church must be reversed.

Covered Up in Worship

Third, the truth of God is being covered up in the worship of the church. The church has been called to praise God "in spirit and truth" (John 4:24). We can worship God only to the extent to which His revealed truth is made known, that is, what He has told us of who He is and what He has done. Jesus said, "God is spirit, and those who worship him must worship in spirit and truth" (v. 24). This means that believers are to worship in their innermost being—in their "spirit"—in the depths of their soul with a proper heart attitude. Moreover, they must do so with the "truth," which renews their minds and inflames their hearts. All true worship must be ignited by and consistent with the revealed Scripture. Doxology is inseparably bound with theology. Our theology inevitably defines our worship. The stronger we are in the Word of God, the stronger we will be in the worship of God.

But when the truth of the divine attributes, works, and names become altered or withheld from the worship service, the adoration of God is undone. When the truth preached and the words sung are superficial, then doxology will be shallow at best and blasphemous at worst. Mindless worship built upon empty ritual and mere emotionalism is not true worship. Whenever this occurs, authentic worship has been downgraded to fleshly responses to man-centered directives.

This is what we are seeing in our day. We have given up the high ground of theology, and we are now standing in the lowlands of mindless theatrics. We have yielded the mountains of sound doctrine and are now standing in the desolate valley of drama and entertainment. Before he died, James Montgomery Boice poignantly wrote, "I hope you have become nauseated with the tawdry entertainment that passes for the true worship of God in many of our churches."[2] It has certainly sickened the head of the church, the Lord Jesus Christ. Countless influences from the world have been brought into the public gathering of the church. When this occurs, the church no longer worships God in truth according to His glory and holiness but merely entertains itself. As long as the church looks to the world to direct its worship rather than to the Word, its worship will always suffer.

2. James Montgomery Boice, *Whatever Happened to the Gospel of Grace? Rediscovering the Doctrines That Shook the World* (Wheaton, Ill.: Crossway, 2009), 65.

Contorted in Ministry

Fourth, the marginalizing of truth in the church is further seen in the ways that the church carries out its ministry. Benjamin Breckenridge Warfield, the Princeton divine, said, "Theology determines our methodology."[3] In our day, our low level of theology is producing a crass methodology in ministry. Pragmatism has become the governing principle in the church. The issue has become what works, not what is true. Thus, many worldly methods drawn from corporate America and marketing schemes are dictating the strategies of many churches. No longer is the guiding light the truth that is taught in Scripture. Instead, we have consulted the world, learned its techniques, and implemented its operational procedures. Our directives are more drawn from the boardrooms of corporate America than from the Pastoral Epistles. Tragically, the church's methods are often devoid of divine wisdom and spiritual discernment, as we have turned from heavenly truth to worldly techniques.

As an example of the crass pragmatism in methodology, the best-selling Christian author and pastor Rick Warren notes, "It is my deep conviction that anybody can be won to Christ if you discover the key to his or her heart."[4] That statement is raw pragmatism, pure and simple. It represents a tragic departure from Paul's visit to Philippi, when God, not Paul, opened Lydia's heart

---

3. Princeton Theological Seminary, *Inauguration of the Rev. Benjamin B. Warfield as Professor of Didactic and Polemic Theology* (New York: Anson D.F. Randolf & Co., 1888), 14.

4. Rick Warren, *The Purpose Driven Church: Growth without Compromising Your Message and Mission* (Grand Rapids, Mich.: Zondervan, 2007), 220.

(Acts 16:14). According to this author, the key that unlocks any person's heart is placed into the hand of the pastor or Christian worker. If you can just discover the key that unlocks that heart, you can open it. That is a long way from a fundamental belief in the truth of sovereign election and effectual calling, which affirms that those whom God has chosen for salvation will be converted to Christ. This crass approach to ministry also contradicts the doctrine of the total depravity of the human heart, which teaches that the heart is locked shut until God alone opens it in regeneration.

Church Growth Amok

This popular book goes on to say that it may take some time to identify what this key is, but the most likely place to start is with the person's felt needs—as opposed to their real need for salvation. The author notes that explosive growth occurs when the type of people in the community match the type of people who are already in the church. This argument follows the line of thinking that like attracts like. If that is so, then lost, carnal people will be attracted to the church only if the congregation is lost and carnal. The straightforward preaching of the Word of God that exalts God, exposes sin, offers Jesus Christ, and calls for repentance and faith is archaic and outdated. Instead, the goal is to make people feel as comfortable in church as possible rather than convicted or challenged.

This is the concealment of truth in the methodology of the church that we are witnessing in this hour. This maddening approach veils the outshining glory of the holiness of God that is to be sent forth from the church. We are neglecting the truth by adopting the ways of the world in an attempt to reach the world. We have forgotten that the church must be *different* from the world in order to make a *difference* in the world.

Contrived in Evangelism

Fifth, the church today is often departing from the truth of God in the work of evangelism. In their attempts to win the lost to Christ, the church has left behind God's Word in both the message presented and the method followed. The one true gospel has been altered by either adding to it or taking away from it. In other words, the pure saving message of Jesus Christ is being changed in order to attract those who stand in dire need of it. When this occurs, the gospel is no longer the power of God unto salvation. Such a gospel becomes "another gospel" (Gal. 1:8–9) that does not save.

This counterfeit gospel is being offered in place of the true gospel. The truth of justification by faith alone is being distorted by what is called the New Perspective on Paul. Here, justification does not occur at the moment of conversion but awaits the last day, depending upon the good works one has performed. The message of being saved from the eternal wrath of God in hell is veiled by the teaching of annihilationism and universalism. The preaching of the lordship of Christ is hidden by the minimalist message of easy-believism that postpones a recognition of the lordship of Christ until a later time. The call to obedience is eclipsed by a hyper-grace antinomianism. The teaching of the holiness of God, which brings deep conviction of sin, has been replaced by a happy God who is never angry with sinners. The radiant glory of sovereign grace has been replaced by the superficiality of raising a hand, walking an aisle, and parroting a prayer in the last five minutes of the church service.

Our First Mission Field

The anemic message and methods of today have caused our churches to become filled with lost, unregenerate church members. There is a great difference between a congregation and a crowd. The latter is primarily a mission field, not a sheepfold. Large numbers are being deceived about their relationship with God. Multitudes profess Christ but do not possess Him. Many come to church but have never come to faith in Jesus Christ. They have been baptized with water but not by the Spirit. They know knowledge about Christ, but they do not actually know Him in their hearts.

New approaches to evangelism hold back the preaching of the law, which is intended to prepare the heart for the gospel by bringing deep conviction of sin. We have silenced the call to repentance and the call to surrender one's life to Jesus Christ. Truth is withheld as people are not told to forsake the world and to entrust themselves to Him who died upon the cross to save sinners.

Veiling of the Truth

This is the veil that is being placed over the truth in many places today. The church is to be "a pillar and buttress of the truth" (1 Tim. 3:15). That is to say, God has entrusted the truth to the church, which is to proclaim and protect it. The church is to hold up the truth before a watching world. The role of teaching and guarding the message of truth is given by God to the church. Countless churches are giving a watered-down Word and worshiping however they desire. Rather than following the teaching of Jesus Christ and His Apostles, the church has turned to techniques, formulas, strategies, and programs.

A full disclosure of the truth must be restored in the churches today. As we honor the truth, the hand of God's blessing will rest upon that ministry. God will honor His truth and nothing else. God will honor the one who honors His Word. May the light of truth shine as never before as we uphold the Word of God.

8

MARGINALIZED TRUTH

The Rejection of Truth in the Christian's Life

In his book *Respectable Sins*, author Jerry Bridges addresses those subtle sins that we, as Christians, often commit, yet consider "acceptable" when compared to other obvious sins that society looks down on. Bridges writes, "Those of us whom I call conservative evangelicals may have become so preoccupied with some of the major sins of society around us that we have lost sight of the need to deal with our own refined or subtle sins."[1] Respectable sins are not blatant sins that are uniformly condemned in others, such as adultery, lying, stealing, embezzlement, drunkenness, or pornography. On the contrary, respectable sins are those we most often tolerate and excuse. We are likely to overlook them because they are not regarded as serious. They are common to everyday

---

1. Jerry Bridges, *Respectable Sins: Confronting the Sins We Tolerate* (Carol Stream, Ill.: Tyndale House, 2014), 9.

life and seen as acceptable, though to a holy God, they are serious and wicked.

Not every sin is the same, of course. The Mosaic law required the death penalty for some transgressions and only restitution for others. Nevertheless, all sin is offensive to God, who is absolutely holy. Every iniquity is a direct violation of the moral purity of His perfect character. Every offense is a flagrant breaking of the moral law of God. In this sense, there are no little sins. Every breaking of the divine standard is a major offense against God. Every trespass is an act of cosmic rebellion against the Lawgiver Himself.

This being so, it is important in the pursuit of holiness that we address even the hidden sins of our own heart attitudes. These are iniquities that we often overlook because we consider them insignificant. But as there are no unimportant people in the kingdom of God, neither are there any inconsequential sins in the life of any believer. Any disobedience to the truth of God's Word must be treated as a serious encroachment against His holy name. God has said, "Be holy, for I am holy" (Lev. 11:44; cf. 19:2; 1 Peter 1:16). This lifelong journey toward personal holiness includes dealing with even the so-called respectable sins. A small fly can contaminate the best ointment. So can those sins that seem small, but in reality are significant, pollute our innermost being.

With this in mind, we want to revisit the second letter that the Apostle Paul addressed to Timothy. This is the last correspondence that we have from the Apostle. In his final challenge, he called Timothy to live a life of personal holiness. With an emphatic pen, Paul wrote his young son in the faith: "Now in a great house there are not only vessels of gold and silver but also of wood and clay, some for honorable use, some for dishonorable. Therefore, if anyone cleanses himself from what is dishonorable, he will be a vessel for honorable use, set apart as holy, useful to the master of the house, ready for every good work" (2 Tim. 2:20–21). Here, Timothy and all believers are likened to these honorable vessels that must be holy in order to be used for honorable purposes. Simply put, God will not use dirty vessels in His house, but those that are pure.

Therefore, all believers are to strive for godliness in order to glorify God and be of utmost use in ministry. For this reason, all sins—even the most seemingly unimportant sins—must be carefully identified and aggressively mortified in the pursuit of holy living. While there are many such respectable sins in our lives, I want us to consider four that are often disregarded: discontentment, impatience, envy, and the misuse of the tongue. Though these are usually not considered offensive to God, they are diametrically contrary to the holiness of God. Moreover, they render us ineffective in our Christian lives. These so-called respectable sins must be removed from our lives, like a deadly cancer from an ailing patient, before they spread and cause greater harm to our souls. They must be treated aggressively, for each one is a disregard of the truth of God.

The Sin of Discontentment

First, we want to examine and expose the respectable sin of discontentment. This revolt against the truth is, in reality, dissatisfaction with God that carries over to unhappiness with one's lot in life. It is a failure to trust Him with where He has placed you and with what He is doing. This is a sin of the heart that is accompanied by other poisonous attitudes such as despondency, discouragement, and unrest. This usually leads to daydreaming about how much better life would be if we were in a different place, in a different position, or with a different person. As time goes on, the discontentment grows and festers in our minds. It is a failure to recognize that God, by His wise providence, has placed us where we are for a reason. Therefore, we are to be content in the will of God, giving ourselves fully to what He has called us to do.

Paul wrote during his first Roman imprisonment, "Not that I am speaking of being in need, for I have learned in whatever situation I am to be content" (Phil. 4:11). Even for the Apostle Paul, the virtue of contentment was not automatic; it had to be learned. When we find ourselves in difficult situations, it is not our natural inclination to be content. Learning to be content in adverse circumstances is instead a supernatural response. Writing while in chains and guarded by Roman soldiers, Paul was waiting to be taken to trial before the mad emperor Nero. Yet, despite this life-threatening situation, we find the vibrant reality of abundant joy flowing from the Apostle's life. Paul calls the believers in Philippi to share in his contentment as they face the difficulties that were being brought their way.

Philippians 4:11 contains the only occurrence of the Greek word (*autarkēs*) in the New Testament; it is translated here as "content." The Greek word carries the idea of "having enough" or "sufficient." It conveys the sense of having sufficient resources to accomplish a task without any need for panic. It means to be independent of the need for additional sources. To be content is not having to be dependent upon others or something else in order to continue successfully. One ancient writer used this word in reference to a country that supplied all its own needs. That is, nothing had to be imported from other countries in order for it to function effectively. In such a scenario, the country possessed all of the necessary natural resources and did not have to rely upon any other nation to supply its needs.

When we trust in the Lord and abide in Him, we find that, like the country with sufficient resources, all our needs are being met in Him. For the Christian, true contentment comes from God, through the abundant grace of the Lord Jesus Christ. Quite simply, contentment is found in our being satisfied in God. Such a spiritual state is realized when we are relying upon His ample resources to meet our needs. When we rest in God, we are at ease in any troublesome time through the vast riches of His grace. True contentment cannot be found in the limited supplies of this fallen, changing world. Nor can it be found in the inadequacies of other people. Instead, true satisfaction is found exclusively in knowing Jesus Christ and in experiencing the fullness of His peace that surpasses all understanding.

Paul shares the secret of experiencing true contentment when he adds, "I can do all things through him who strengthens me" (Phil. 4:13). This comprehensive statement refers to "all things" that are lawful. That is, he means all those things that glorify God, promote His kingdom, and exalt His Son. Despite the demanding circumstances of life, Paul learned this invaluable lesson of relying upon the all-sufficient grace of the

Lord Jesus Christ, which enabled him to do all things within the will of God.

Elsewhere, Paul writes, "If we have food and clothing, with these we will be content" (1 Tim. 6:8). "Content" here conveys the idea of being satisfied with what God provides. "Food and clothing" refers to the basic necessities of life, which should be enough to make us content. There is certainly nothing wrong with possessing things. But what is wrong is not being satisfied with what God has provided. The Apostle also writes, "I am content with weaknesses, insults, hardships, persecutions, and calamities" (2 Cor. 12:10). Here, a different word for "content" (Greek *eudokeō*) means "to be well pleased with, to take pleasure in." Even when he experienced weakness, insults, distresses, persecutions, and difficulties, Paul was content because when he was weak, then he was strong. Paul writes, "Godliness with contentment is great gain" (1 Tim. 6:6).

Whatever secret of contentment that Paul has learned, we must learn it as well. If our inner peace depends upon other people or the circumstances of life, we will be living on an emotional roller-coaster. If that is the case, when our happenings are good, then our happiness will be good. But when our dealings are adverse, then our emotional state will be riding low. However, if our contentment is truly found in God, a supernatural joy will abide despite the adverse events around us. Like the Apostle Paul, this is a lesson we must all learn.

From these verses, we may rightly surmise that trusting in the flesh is a respectable sin. We are often tempted to lean upon anything or anyone except the Lord Jesus Christ. Discontentment results from a failure to look to Christ, and instead our gaze becomes fixated upon our difficult circumstances. This reality is vividly portrayed when Peter asked the Lord Jesus that he might come to Him while finding himself in a storm on the Sea of Galilee. As long as he had his eyes upon Jesus Christ, he was divinely enabled to walk upon water. However, as the waves crashed around him, his focus then shifted to the threatening circumstances. He began to sink and panicked, crying out, "Lord, save me" (Matt. 14:30). In that moment, the Lord reached out and pulled him up. At once, Peter was safe in the boat with Jesus.

This often pictures our own lives in our moments of truth. We want to walk with the Lord, and we seem to be doing well. But when the storms come, we fix upon the circumstantial waves that are crashing all around us. In that moment, we begin to sink emotionally and drown in a sea of despair. We think that if we were only in some other setting, everything would be so much better. Yet what we truly need is to keep our eyes upon the Lord Jesus Christ regardless of what is threatening us. The author of Hebrews knew this truth and wrote: "looking to Jesus, the founder and perfecter of our faith" (Heb. 12:2). The more we look to Jesus, the stronger our faith becomes, and only then the better we can guard ourselves against discontentment.

Jesus Christ called us to this contentment when He said, "be content with your wages" (Luke 3:14). In other words, we must trust Him to meet our needs. This is yet another Greek word for "to be content," *arkeō*, which means "to be of unfailing strength." The idea is to be satisfied or content with what one possesses. The author of Hebrews instructs believers, "Be content with what you have" (Heb. 13:5). "To be content" (*arkeō*) means "to be satisfied with." Contentment is realized when we put our trust in the Lord and not anyone or anything else. When we are discouraged, it is inevitably because our focus has been removed from the Lord, and we are not looking to Him as we should. Being content means that we are satisfied with Jesus Christ and who we are in Him, with what He has given us, and with the circumstances in which He has placed us.

Believers need this true contentment in life. We need the supernatural calm that comes only when we trust that God has providentially placed us where we are. It is here that we learn His resources are all-sufficient and at our disposal. Let us learn that God is greater than anything that would overwhelm us. He alone can give us stability in the storms of life and a peace that surpasses all comprehension. In his classic work *The Rare Jewel of Christian Contentment,* Puritan author Jeremiah Borroughs wrote: "Christian contentment is that sweet, inward, quiet, gracious frame of spirit which freely submits to and delights in God's wise and fatherly disposal in every condition."[2] This inner tranquility is what the Lord gives to those who abide in Him.

Are you at peace in your heart in your present circumstances? Or are you restless? Are you searching for that elusive something? Do you want to be anywhere but where God has placed you? It is a respectable sin to be discontent when we have the abundant

---

2. Jeremiah Burroughs, *The Rare Jewel of Christian Contentment* (1648; repr. Lafayette, Ind.: Sovereign Grace, 2001), 2.

sufficiency of God's grace at our disposal. Perhaps one of the greatest needs in your life is a renewed commitment to be where God has called you, where you are.

This is not to say that God would never move you to a different setting. But let us remember that for the moment, God uses adversity to mature and conform us into the very image of Jesus Christ. He is the Lord of the storm, and He often sends His disciples into the tempests of life in the darkest hour of the night, so that He might develop and deepen our faith. So He does with you and me as well. Let us learn the lessons that He has intended for us.

The Sin of Impatience

Second, closely related to discontentment is the respectable sin of impatience. Though this seemingly small sin often appears insignificant, impatience is in reality the failure to wait upon God in our lives. Impatience comes when we become restless and grow tired of waiting for God to answer our prayers. As a result, we act impulsively and take matters into our own hands. We then move ahead of God, which is a dangerous thing to do. Impatience becomes the breeding ground for other sins such as agitation, anxiety, and irritability.

The impatience of God's people is seen all throughout Scripture as a sin that inevitably leads to other sins. We are familiar with the impatience of the patriarch Abraham and his wife, Sarah. In their old age, God promised them that they would have a son. Sarah laughed when she heard this divine revelation. Though they received the promise, they became weary of waiting for God to act. So they took matters into their own hands and produced an offspring of their own doing, Ishmael. They were to wait for the son of promise, Isaac, but they became impatient and suffered for it in the end. They would have to wait many years to see its fulfillment; the writer of Hebrews tells us that, "having patiently waited, [he] obtained the promise" (Heb. 6:15). So must you and I learn to wait on the Lord.

During the wilderness wanderings of Israel, the children of God became impatient with Him because their journey to the Promised Land was taking longer than they desired. Their restlessness caused them to rebel against God. "The people became impatient on the way" (Num. 21:4). This literally reads, "The soul of the people was short." This is to say, they were short of patience with God. They should have been long-suffering, enduring, and persevering, but they were not. They wanted the journey to the Promised Land to progress faster than it was. When their wilderness wanderings did not end quickly, they became impatient with God. The text continues, "And the people spoke against God and against Moses, 'Why have you brought us up out of Egypt to die in the wilderness?'" (Num. 21:5). A spirit of impatience provoked this carnal cry, demanding an answer from Moses with an immediate solution. This impatience soon led to anger and frustration toward God and His chosen leader. Little did they realize that the cause of the delay lay with themselves.

Wait for the Lord

The prophet Isaiah said much the same when he maintained that believers must "wait for the LORD" (Isa. 40:31). This word "wait" carries the idea of a positive, expectant hope while remaining in a holding position. In other words, believers are to wait for the Lord while positively anticipating that He will work in due time. This kind of waiting upon God is an act of great confidence. Those who wait for the Lord are patiently expecting God's perfect timing. In the meantime, they are bearing up under great difficultly. They will not act impulsively and forge ahead of God. Instead, they will delay moving ahead until God's appointed time is realized in their lives. God most often moves methodically in our lives as He aims to grow our faith over an extended period of time.

Isaiah characterizes those who wait for the Lord as those who "shall renew their strength" (Isa. 40:31). The idea is that of exchanging their finite weakness for His infinite strength. Conversely, those who are impatient with God will inevitably be worn out and grow weary as they live their lives. But as they wait for the Lord, the prophet adds, "they shall mount up with wings like eagles." They will soar above their difficulties as they rest in the Lord. But those who act impulsively and operate by their own schedules will be grounded in their trials and never sprout wings and fly. Further, Isaiah says, "They shall run and not be weary; they shall walk and not faint." The reason they do not become weary is because they are walking in the strength that God supplies. When we do not wait on the Lord, we are walking in our own strength. But when we choose to wait on God, He bears us up with supernatural strength.

The Scriptures frequently speak of how necessary it is that we wait on God. The psalmist David repeatedly urges us to not get ahead of God: "I waited patiently for the LORD; he inclined to me and heard my cry" (Ps. 40:1). God is most attentive to the cry of a waiting soul. He turns His ear to hear their plea for help. Again, David writes, "None who wait for you shall be put to shame" (Ps. 25:3). There are no exceptions to this assertion. All who wait upon the Lord will never be disappointed. David adds, "For you I wait all day long" (Ps. 25:5). Such patience often involves waiting for an extended delay. Further, the psalmist adds, "Wait for the LORD; be strong, and let your heart take courage; wait for the LORD!" (Ps. 27:14). In other words, it requires courage to wait upon God when one is surrounded by mounting dangers. David also urges, "Be still before the LORD and wait patiently for him. . . . Wait for the LORD and keep his way" (Ps. 37:7, 34).

The Apostle Paul addresses the need for waiting upon God when he lists that the fruit of the spirit includes "patience" (Gal. 5:22). "Patience" (Greek *makrothumia*) refers to long-suffering that endures the harm inflicted by others. It is a calm willingness to accept difficult situations that are painful or irritating. Waiting for the Lord requires a willingness to accept and endure painful situations until God changes the circumstance. The respectable sin of being impatient must be fought against and put to death in our lives.

Paul also charges believers to be patient. He writes, "Put on then, as God's chosen ones, holy and beloved, compassionate hearts, . . . patience" (Col. 3:12). This verb is in the present tense and imperative mood. In other words, we are commanded to always be putting on patience in every situation of life. This implies the natural tendency of our flesh is to act impulsively. This Apostolic command requires that we must obey as a choice of our will to be patient, in full reliance upon His enabling power. Paul also writes that we must be walking "with patience, bearing with one another in love" (Eph. 4:2). The Apostle instructs us to be long-suffering in the negative circumstances of life and act out of love.

The Sin of Envy

Third, we must watch out for another respectable sin, namely, envy. Envy is an evil desire to possess what belongs to someone else. The Greek word translated "envy" (*phthonos*) means "ill will, jealousy, spite." This sin involves a hateful attitude toward others because of what they possess. In turn, it produces an additional feeling of displeasure with our own lot in life. This sin is provoked by hearing of the advantage or prosperity of others to the exclusion of what we do not have. John MacArthur writes, "By definition, the envious person cannot be satisfied with what he has and will always crave for more."[3] Envy is summed up in the proverb, "The leech has two daughters: Give and Give. Three things are never satisfied; four never say, 'Enough'" (Prov. 30:15). Simply put, envy never has enough.

3. John MacArthur, *Titus*, The MacArthur New Testament Commentary (Chicago: Moody, 1986), 149.

In the Old Testament, we see a clear example of the sin of envy in the narrative of Joseph and his older brothers in Genesis 37. Joseph was the youngest son of Jacob and was beloved and quite spoiled by him. Joseph's brothers could not bear to see their youngest brother treated in this favored way and were envious of him. As Joseph shared miraculous dreams of ruling over his brothers, their envy grew deeper. This envy soon turned into an intense jealousy and even hatred toward Joseph. The brothers conspired against him, desiring to kill him, but instead kidnapped him and sold him into slavery. Though these horrible acts were clearly wrong and Joseph would suffer for many years in a foreign land, God ultimately used this for good, saving a nation through Joseph's life.

In this story, we see how the sin of envy can grow into an intense hatred, even manifesting itself into wicked deeds and acts. Envy seeks only its own good and disregards the needs of those whom we are called to love. Selfishness and a desire for what others possess will continue to fester and grow, sometimes even unseen by others, until it has a stronghold in a person's heart. We must be careful to examine our hearts for this respectable sin and repent of it whenever it is discovered. We must turn from this sin as we seek to have a pure heart before the Lord.

The Apostle Peter addresses this sin when he writes, "So, put away all . . . envy" (1 Peter 2:1). Envy is a respectable sin that all believers must consciously lay aside. Envy denotes the attitude of those who resent the prosperity of others, and that often leads to grudges, bitterness, hatred, and conflict with them. This respectable sin is the desire to deprive others of what is rightfully theirs, to wish that they did not have it or had it to a lesser degree. Envy is wishing they did not have what they have, and it includes jealousy, which is wanting what others possess. Most often, envy leads to strife and conflict with other brothers and sisters in Christ.

Exposing this same sin, James writes, "You covet and cannot obtain; so you fight and quarrel" (James 3:2). No matter what a person has, the flesh will always crave for more. Whatever one has is never enough for one's sinful flesh. These sinful desires for more are insatiable and can consume a person. The flesh cannot tolerate another person having what it does not have. Nor can it stand for someone to have more of something or better than what it has. Such a person will always want more or better than he has, no matter how good his situation is or how much he has. The Apostle Paul warns against "envy" (1 Tim. 6:4). This respectable sin is the inward discontent over the benefits or popularity enjoyed by others. It is accompanied by "dissension, slander, evil suspicions, and constant friction" (vv. 4–5). By this, we see that envy leads to all kinds of other sins. Envy marks every life before one comes to faith in Jesus Christ. Paul writes, "For we ourselves were once foolish . . . passing our days in malice and envy" (Titus 3:3). He lists envy as a work of the flesh (Gal. 5:21) in which we once lived.

Jerry Bridges writes, "We tend to envy those first with whom we most closely identify, and second, in those areas we value most."[4] Envy must be uprooted out of our hearts

4. Bridges, *Respectable Sins*, 149.

with radical repentance, or it will devour us. Either we put to death the sin of envy or it will kill us. There can be no truce with envy, no peaceful coexistence. As you look inward, is God revealing seeds of envy that have established a hold in your heart? Is there a wrong desire or displeasure toward the success of others? Whatever is there, deal with it aggressively. Be at peace with the sovereignty of God in your life. Be focused upon the Lord Jesus Christ. Rest in His all-wise provision in your life.

The Sin of the Tongue

Fourth, one last respectable sin that we want to consider is the misuse of the tongue. Many sins of the mouth are obviously dishonoring to God. But certain sins involving the use of our speech are too often considered to be acceptable. This inappropriate use of the tongue involves certain forms of humor that are expressed at the expense of others. It also includes various forms of sarcasm that put others down. This also takes into account instances of gossip, self-flattery, and self-promotion, in which we elevate ourselves rather than clothing our speech with humility. Each of these respectable sins of the tongue must be removed from our mouth.

In no uncertain terms, Paul says, "Let no corrupting talk come out of your mouths" (Eph. 4:29). This word translated "corrupting" (Greek *sapros*) means "foul" and was used to describe rotten food or spoiled, even putrefied, fruit. In essence, Paul is saying that nothing should come out of a believer's mouth that is inconsistent with the holy character of God and His high calling upon our lives. We must not allow any corrupting words to come from our mouths. Instead, we must speak "only such as is good for building up, as fits the occasion, that it may give grace to those who hear. And do not grieve the Holy Spirit of God" (Eph. 4:29–30). When we misuse our tongues, we grieve the Spirit who resides within us because we are tearing down others rather than building them up.

In addressing the use of the tongue, Paul says in the next chapter, "Let there be no filthiness nor foolish talk nor crude joking, which are out of place, but instead let there be thanksgiving" (Eph. 5:4). "Filthiness" (Greek *aischrotēs*) refers to that which is degrading, disgraceful, and shameful. Such talk should never proceed from our lips. It may be respectable in many circles, even popular, but it is rejected by heaven.

When Paul forbids "foolish talk," he means that form of speech that is dull or stupid. The Greek word, *mōrologia*, is a compound that joins together *mōros*, from which we derive the English word *moron*, and *legō*, which means "to say, to speak out." The word describes stupid talk that belongs to someone who is intellectually deficient. It is a lewd obscenity that has no point except to pollute others. "Coarse jesting" (Greek *eutrapelia*) joins together *eu*, meaning "well, good," with *tropē*, meaning "a turning." It describes speech that uses nimbleness of wit, or quickness in making repartee. This refers to dirty language and suggestive innuendos with double entendres and dirty stories.

Such words may be good for a laugh, but they hinder our growth in godliness. Moreover, they can be hurtful and even devastating to others. Our mouths can so easily corrupt the influence of our lives on others. The Bible says, "If anyone does not stumble in what he says, he is a perfect man, able also to bridle his whole body" (James 3:2). In saying "perfect," James is speaking of maturity, as of a full-grown adult. The idea is to reach a level of completeness in the faith, though not sinless perfection. One who cannot bridle his tongue is not mature in Christ.

Jesus Christ spoke with words that were always sensitive to the occasion. It was prophesied of the Messiah, "He will not cry aloud or lift up his voice, or make it heard in the street; a bruised reed he will not break, and a faintly burning wick he will not quench; he will faithfully bring forth justice" (Isa. 42:2–3). To those who had been trampled under by the blows of life, He said, "Your sins are forgiven" (Luke 7:48). He did not break a bruised reed with harsh words. Yet when it came to the hard-hearted religious leaders, He sternly rebuked them: "Woe to you, scribes and Pharisees, hypocrites! For you are like white-washed tombs" (Matt. 23:27). We also should use our mouths to encourage others in their pursuit of holiness. We must measure our words carefully that they be "seasoned with salt" (Col. 4:6). The proper use of our tongues consists in not only what we say, but how we say it. Let us make sure we are "speaking the truth in love" (Eph. 4:15). As we speak the truth, the tone and trajectory of our conversation must be loving, under the influence of the Holy Spirit.

Search Me, O God

These four respectable sins demand our most careful scrutiny and repentance. Though not condemned by many as sins to be dealt with aggressively, these sins must nevertheless be confronted and confessed. These are sins, often tolerated, that must be terminated as long as we live in this world. Even respectable sins are sins that can ruin one's walk before the Lord. If the truth is to be lived out in our lives, these sins must be removed by the grace of God.

David writes, "Search me, O God" (Ps. 139:23). The word translated "search" is the same word used of Joshua and Caleb when they ventured into the Promised Land to spy on its condition. They carefully explored the land in order to give an accurate report. Likewise, believers must submit to the guiding light of the Holy Spirit, the Word of God, and our consciences. We invite God to search our hearts and reveal to us any of these respectable sins. God already knew David's heart. What David prayed is that God would reveal to him his own heart, for unless God made it known to him, he would not correctly know his own heart. We are so often self-deceived about our own motives and spirituality. We so often are experts on the sins of others, yet remain blind to our own iniquities.

We must pursue this purity of heart and life. We must desire to rid ourselves of every respectable sin, so that we would be honorable vessels, used by God for His own purposes. Can you imagine a surgeon, in the middle of a procedure, dropping his scalpel on the ground, picking it up, wiping it off with his sweaty scrubs and applying the instrument to the patient's heart or brain? This would be unimaginable. How much more will the Great Physician prioritize personal holiness in those servants whom He would use in this world? God will surely reach for those clean instruments—servants who are confessing and repenting of their sin. These are the ones whom the Lord uses.

May the Holy Spirit have this sanctifying effect upon every part of our bodies. May we be pure and clean instruments, useful to the Lord's work in the building of His kingdom. May we ask God to make each one of us more like Christ because, in reality, there are no respectable sins, for all sins are a rejection of the truth and an offense to God. May we be repenters of any sin in our lives as we seek to love and honor the Lord with our lives.

Part 3

THE REIGN
OF TRUTH

9

PREACHING THE TRUTH

The Reign of Truth in the Expository Pulpit

Dr. Martyn Lloyd-Jones, the famed expositor of Westminster Chapel in London, delivered a series of lectures on preaching at Westminster Theological Seminary in which he stated: "The most urgent need in the Christian church today is true preaching. As it is the greatest and most urgent need in the church, it is the greatest need of the world also."[1] If the Doctor's diagnosis is correct, and I believe it is, then biblical preaching remains the greatest need in the church today, as well as in the world. If a reformation is to come to the church, it must begin in the pulpit. As the pulpit goes, so goes the church, and as the church goes, so goes its influence upon the world.

The prophet Amos warned of a coming time in his day that would cover the land with a famine, not of food, but for

---

1. D. Martyn Lloyd-Jones, *Preaching and Preachers* (Grand Rapids, Mich.: Zondervan, 1972), 9.

hearing the word of the Lord. Theologian Walter C. Kaiser Jr. is among many who have declared that this famine is now here in full force. Kaiser writes, "The famine of the word continues in massive proportions in most parts of North America."[2] We are indeed living in days of spiritual drought, a time when the church is starved for truth. Now more than ever, pastors must proclaim the truth by returning to their highest and primary calling—the divine summons to preach the Word.

The Apostle Paul issued this call to Timothy, and to all pastors down through the centuries, in 2 Timothy 4:1–5. What this veteran preacher had to say to his young son in the ministry is of utmost importance to all who are called by God to stand behind a pulpit and preach. The first business of the church is preaching the Word. Therefore, it is the first business of the preacher. The importance of biblical preaching cannot be overstated, for no church will rise any higher than its pulpit. A strong pulpit inevitably leads to a strong church, but conversely, a weak pulpit will always lead to a weak church. As the pulpit goes, so goes the church.

These words in 2 Timothy 4 are the last divinely inspired correspondence that the Apostle Paul wrote. These words bring to conclusion a lifetime of ministry by the Apostle. As such, they call for our strictest and most careful attention. They are found in the climactic position of Paul's thirteen epistles, the crescendo of all that he had received from God to give to the church. Last words should be lasting words for young Timothy and for us.

2. Walter Kaiser Jr., *Revive Us Again* (Nashville, Tenn.: B&H, 1999), 166–67.

Writing from Death Row

Paul wrote this final epistle around AD 67. According to tradition, he was imprisoned in the Mamertine Prison in Rome, where he was held captive in a hole in the ground. No light entered this dark prison, save for a small circle at the top through which food was dropped. No sanitation was available. It was pitch black and cold, and the Apostle was there virtually alone as he penned his last correspondence with the outside world. Only Luke was with him. This was no time to mince words or talk about secondary matters. This moment of truth demanded that he address his young protégé with this subject of greatest significance in ministry. We can hear the passion of his heart as his words echo through the corridors of time: "Timothy," he says, "this is the last thing I will ever say to you: Preach the Word."

What Paul wrote to Timothy, he says to every man who is called by God to preach the Word. Further, it addresses the kind of church of which every believer needs to be a part. Either you must preach the Word as Paul prescribes here or you must be under this kind of preaching. Tragically, many believers languish by not being under the influence of such biblical preaching. But nevertheless, this is the divine standard. What Paul outlines in these verses is God's design for a healthy church and dynamic Christian living and ministry.

The Seriousness of the Charge

In these strong words, we first see the *seriousness* of the charge to preach the Word. Paul begins in 2 Timothy 4:1 by saying, "I charge you." This whole passage is given in the form of an Apostolic charge. The word translated "charge" (Greek *diamarturomai*) was a word drawn from the military world and was used by a commanding officer issuing orders to a subordinate. Here, it carries the force of an order from an authoritative Apostle to a lesser servant of the Lord, an order that is binding upon the lesser servant's life. These words are not mere suggestions for Timothy to consider on how to conduct his ministry. Nor are they helpful hints from the elder Apostle for Timothy to ponder and choose as he pleases. Rather, this is a solemn charge from a commanding officer to one who is lower in rank. By implication, this extends to every pastor who hears these words, "I charge you."

If this were not enough to grab Timothy by the lapels and draw him up in his seat, Paul then adds, "in the presence of God and of Christ Jesus" (v. 1). In reality, this Apostolic charge comes from God Himself and Jesus Christ. Paul is simply the mouthpiece for this charge. This command does not originate with him but is merely passed on by him. This directive has come down from the very throne of God, the sovereign God who rules and reigns over all. It originated with God in heaven and now comes down through Paul to Timothy. It comes with binding force from the Lord Jesus Christ, who appeared to Paul on the Damascus Road in the blinding light of the shekinah glory of God, who literally knocked him to the ground. Jesus sovereignly arrested Saul and summoned him to Himself and into gospel ministry. This very same Jesus Christ now issues this charge through the Apostle to Timothy, and now to us.

Every Preacher's Accountability

Paul further tightens the sobriety of this charge by reminding Timothy that Jesus Christ is the one "who is to judge the living and the dead" (2 Tim. 4:1). Paul makes it abundantly clear that it is Christ who will judge every preacher on the last day, when each man will give an account of himself to Jesus as a servant to his master. For this reason, the Bible says, "Not many of you should become teachers, my brothers, for you know that we who teach will be judged with greater strictness" (James 3:1). Jesus said, "Everyone to whom much was given, of him much will be required" (Luke 12:48). A great stewardship has been entrusted to the preacher in his commission to preach the Word. Thus, more is required of him than of other men. Pastors have been set apart by God to devote themselves to prayer and the study of the Word of God (Acts 6:4). Thus, pastors are to be workers who need not be ashamed, accurately handling of the Word of God (2 Tim. 2:15). They must cut it straight with the Scripture and answer for it to God and Jesus Christ.

This accountability is heightened when Paul writes, "For we must all appear before the judgment seat of Christ, so that each one may receive what is due for what he has done in the body, whether good or evil" (2 Cor. 5:10). It is this coming day of judgment before Jesus Christ that Paul has in mind as he writes to Timothy. Each preacher must lay the right foundation in ministry, preaching Jesus Christ. He must build upon it with great care, as each one's work will be revealed by fire on the final day (1 Cor. 3:10–15). There will be a reward for those preachers who build upon it with gold, silver, and precious stones. They must preach the right message with the right methods and the right motives. But those who go through all the activities of ministry and engage in all the routines of shepherding the flock, but who do not rightly handle the Word of God nor bring it in the prescribed manner, are building with wood, hay, and stubble. The last day will reveal it, as the entirety of that ministry will go up in flames in a moment. Such preachers will be saved, yet so as through fire.

This climactic scene vividly illustrates the seriousness of expository preaching. Stepping into the pulpit in order to speak for God is no time to mess around. This task is not for one who is uncalled, untaught, and unprepared. Simply put, this is no time for amateur hour. Jesus Christ will have a far stricter judgment for each one who steps forward to speak His Word.

Paul concludes his introduction by referring to "his appearing and his kingdom." He concludes by referencing the appearing of Jesus Christ, the second coming of our Lord. When the Lord comes back, the preacher will directly give an account to the One who called him regarding how he handled His Word. How seriously every preacher must take his call to preach. It is incumbent upon each pastor that he be a God-fearing man. He must hold with the greatest humility this sovereign call to preach the Word. He must always remember that there is a final day when he will stand before the Lord and give an account of how he used his life in the proclamation of the Word of God.

The Substance of the Charge

Having established the seriousness of preaching, Paul moves on to the substance of his charge. The Apostle details how the charge is to be carried out by issuing nine imperative commands. The overall substance of what he has to say is found in this first imperative: "Preach the word" (2 Tim. 4:2). The remaining eight imperatives describe how Timothy is to preach. He concludes at the end of verse 5 by saying, "Fulfill your ministry." Everything that follows "Preach the word" regulates how the pastor is to preach the Word in order to fulfill his ministry.

These nine imperatives come in rapid, staccato fashion, and it is important not to miss any of them. All nine commands are important. This is not a multiple choice in which Timothy is free to select three or four commands that he would like to follow. Paul's charge requires that all nine imperatives be obeyed.

Paul begins by charging Timothy, "Preach the word." This command is based upon the seriousness of the charge. The word "preach" translates the Greek *kērussō*, which means "to herald, to publicly proclaim." In New Testament times, a king would dispatch a herald as an official royal messenger. He was sent by the initiative of the ruling monarch and would go to the outer perimeters of the kingdom. There, he was to do but one thing: he was to represent the *kurios*, the lord, the king upon his throne. He had no message except what had been entrusted to him. He had no duty but to speak what had been given to him. He was a royal spokesman sent to issue a proclamation. He was not to chat with the people as he shared this message or to dialogue about it in a casual fashion. Rather, he was to declare it directly as it was given.

There is a noble dignity about this word *preach*, as the preacher represents the sovereign throne of the universe. This is no time for joke-telling, clowning around, entertaining people, or courting popularity. Instead, he is to be a divinely dispatched ambassador who represents the high throne of heaven.

The preacher is to speak as one who has been sent from God to preach *the* Word. The definite article "the" tells us there is only one message that he is to bring. It is *the* Word of the living God, not *a* word from any other source. He is to bring the entirety of *the* Word in the full counsel of God.

The Reformers had several Latin slogans that gripped their hearts, one of which was *sola Scriptura*, meaning "Scripture alone." They had nothing else to say. Another was *tota Scriptura*, meaning they were to preach all of Scripture.

Stay in the Text

Several synonyms are used by Paul in 2 Timothy for "the word." In 3:16, the Word is referred to as "Scripture." That is the Greek word *graphē*, which means "the writings," all of which were inspired by God and written down to be recognized as Scripture. In 3:15, the Word is referred to as "the sacred writings," meaning they are holy writings, pure and undefiled, like no other book. In 2:15, the Word is referred to as the "word of truth," which indicates how the Scripture always speaks divine truth. In 2:9, it is called the "word of God," meaning it is the Word that has proceeded from God. In 2:5, the image of the athlete is used to indicate that the Word is the "rules," or the instructions by which the game of life is to be played. In 1:13, it is called the "pattern of the sound words," the reference point by which all is measured. In 4:13, it is referenced as "the books," the papyrus rolls of the Old Testament, or the "parchments" that contain the Scripture.

Timothy is to have nothing to say apart from the Word of God. He is to be a man of one Book, the Bible. His preaching is not to be filled with moral dissertations, political agendas, personal opinions, worldly philosophies, or religious traditions. When Timothy opens his mouth, he must speak only the Word of God. This is what expository preaching is. This word *expository* relates to setting forth meaning or purpose. The idea is to set forth the meaning of a text of Scripture or give a presentation of the principal themes and the theology in a passage. It means an explanation, a commentary, or an exposure of the meaning of the Word. What expository preaching does is explain the divine authorial intent of a passage of Scripture and what its implications are for life.

John MacArthur has well said, "The meaning of the text is the text."[3] That is to say, until you have the meaning of the text, you do not have the text. All you have is black print on white paper. Through the laws of hermeneutics, which is the science of interpretation, pastors must determine the one, true, God-given interpretation of a passage of Scripture and discover how it fits

3. See *The MacArthur Study Bible,* NASB ed., ed. John F. MacArthur (Nashville, Tenn.: Thomas Nelson, 2013), xxvii–xxix.

with the overall message of the Bible. When the preacher stands to preach, he is to explain what this passage meant to the author who wrote it and how the original recipients understood it. So often today in small group Bible study, the leader will say something like this: "What does this text mean to you?" However, it matters not what the text means to man. Rather, the fundamental issue is what did the author mean by what he said. This is the primary role of the expositor. He must wrestle out of the Bible the true meaning of the text.

Expositors Must Preach

The word *expository* must be inseparably joined with the word *preaching*. If a sermon is expository in substance, but not preaching in delivery, it will be cerebral and cognitive. On the other hand, if the message is preaching but no exposition, then the preacher simply has become loud. The preacher must be both expository and preaching. One without the other is always deficient. The Puritans used to explain that there must be a fire in the pulpit. A fire produces both light and heat. So it must be in the pulpit. There must be the light of illumination with the heat of passion and zeal. There must be what the text means with how it is delivered. Only expository preaching emits both light and heat.

Preaching involves more than simply the transfer of information. Preaching stands on the shoulders of teaching and reaches higher. It must have the truth of teaching but be delivered with the dynamics of a public proclamation of the message. Preaching includes motivation, inspiration, application, exhortation, consolation, edification, confrontation, conviction, correction, persuasion, affirmation, and edification. All of these are necessary elements in bringing the Word of God to bear upon the lives of the listeners.

Martyn Lloyd-Jones called preaching "theology on fire."[4] That is, expository preaching comes when a text of Scripture blazes in the heart of the preacher. It is preaching that issues from a man who is on fire with the truth. It is preaching that shines forth with the light of illumination and explanation, yet with the heat of passion, motivation, consolation, edification, and more.

Expository preaching starts with a text of Scripture, stays with a text throughout the entire message, and supports it with other texts. The preacher moves consecutively through a text of Scripture while explaining and applying it. That is the genius of expository preaching. The pastor reads, explains, and applies the text.

The Dynamics of Preaching

I must issue a word of warning here. Many people react against the idea of expository preaching because they have sat under lifeless lectures that bear no resemblance to expository preaching other than name alone. Expository preaching is no license to be boring. Expository preaching is not a data dump in the pulpit. It is not an encyclopedia lecture. It must come with passion, or it is not actual preaching.

---

4. Lloyd-Jones, *Preaching and Preachers*, 97.

There will be introductions, transitions, illustrations, and conclusions, all of it woven together to make one beautiful tapestry that presents the truth. As John Stott said, "We stand between two worlds."[5] With one hand, a pastor touches the ancient world of the biblical author, and with the other hand, he touches the contemporary world of his listeners. He becomes the bridge that connects the ancient text to the modern listener, and as such, he must have his hands upon both worlds as he preaches the Word of God.

In expository preaching, the pastor is to address the entire person of his listeners—the mind, the emotion, and the will. He seeks to illumine and instruct their minds with the truth, inspire and ignite their hearts with a love for the truth and a hatred of their sin, and invite and impel their wills to commit to the truth that has been presented. To put it in another way, expository preaching enlightens and explains the meaning of the text to the mind, inflames and enlarges the affections in the heart, and encourages and enlists the will.

John Calvin wrote regarding expository preaching, "It is the explication of Scripture unfolding its natural and true meaning, while making application to the life experience of the congregation."[6] That is the heart of expository preaching, and that is the summons of expository preaching. It matters

5. John Stott, *Between Two Worlds: The Art of Preaching in the Twentieth Century* (Grand Rapids, Mich.: Eerdmans, 1982), 7.

6. Cited in John H. Leigh, "Calvin's Doctrine of the Proclamation of the Word and Its Significance for Today in the Light of Recent Research," *Review and Expositor* 86 (1989): 32, 34.

to God how the pastor preaches. It matter to God how His Word is handled. It matters to God how His Word is brought before His people.

The Specifics of the Charge

This leads to the specifics of expository preaching, and how the Word is to be preached. Following the command to "preach the word" (2 Tim. 4:2) are eight further imperatives. Every one of these is timeless, transcendent, and binding upon the conscience of every preacher. No one can step outside of these eight imperatives, and to walk away from these eight imperatives is to abandon one's call. The pastor is not allowed to play fast and loose with the Word of God. No man is allowed to reinvent preaching nor preach however he chooses. He must comply with what Paul specifies here in Scripture.

First, Paul says, "Be ready in season and out of season" (2 Tim. 4:2). This carries the idea of alertness, preparation, readiness, and urgency, always being ready to preach the Word of God. The word "ready" was used of a soldier being prepared to go into battle at a moment's notice. His sword was to be always pulled from his sheath and ready to be thrust.

"In season and out of season" is a colloquial expression that means "all the time." There is no season other than in season or out of season. Paul is saying that Timothy is to preach the Word all the time, when it is convenient and when it is not convenient, when it is welcomed and when it is not welcomed, when it is well received and when it is not well received. There is never a time when the Word of God is out of place. It is to be preached in good times and in bad times, throughout the entirety of the pastor's ministry.

Reprove and Rebuke

Second, Paul says, "reprove" (2 Tim. 4:2). The word "reprove" carries the idea of exposing sin. When the pastor preaches the Word of God, he is to expose sin in the lives of his listeners. This refers to bringing sin out into the open and exposing it for what it is: a rebellion against God Himself, a violation of God's holiness, and an insurrection against God's sovereignty. It involves naming sin, confronting sin, and exposing sin for what it is. Sin must be brought home to the listener's conscience before he can repent.

Third, Paul commands Timothy to "rebuke." After sin has been brought into the light and exposed as sin through reproving, then the listener must be brought under conviction of sin and warned of its dangers and consequences. The word "rebuke" carries the idea of a "threatening command," usually with negative implications for the one being rebuked. All true preaching must have this confrontational element, and we see this exemplified by Jesus in the Sermon on the Mount. In Matthew 5:22, He says, "Everyone who is angry with his brother will be liable to judgment; whoever insults his brother will be liable to the council; and whoever says, 'You fool!' will be liable to the hell of fire." That is what reproving and rebuking does: it exposes sin, and it warns the listener.

Exhort with Patience

The fourth imperative in this unfolding series is to "exhort" (2 Tim. 4:2). The Greek word translated here (*parakaleō*) means "to come alongside another," and what a beautiful balance this is. Not only do pastors reprove and rebuke, which have a confrontational element, but they also come alongside the listener, almost as if putting an arm around him, in order to comfort, console, and counsel. In other passages of Scripture, the word "exhort" carries the idea of encouragement. The idea is of lifting up the downcast, firing up the discouraged, and holding up the weak. As it relates to preaching, this means that pastors are to renew their listeners with hope, refresh them with the truth of God's grace, and revive and restore them with the message. They are to come alongside the flock as they preach the Word in order to encourage them to look up to God.

This dual practice of confrontation and exhortation is manifested in Paul's words to the Thessalonian church where he said, "But we were gentle among you, like a nursing mother taking care of her own children" (1 Thess. 2:7), and then a few sentences later, "For you know how, like a father with his children, we exhorted each one of you and encouraged you and charged you to walk in a manner worthy of God" (vv. 11–12). In other words, pastors are to have the gentleness of a mother and a strictness of a father. They must put both arms around the listener in this manner.

The Apostle Paul amplifies that this exhortation must be done "with complete patience" (2 Tim. 4:2). The word "patience," (Greek *makrothumia*), refers to being long-suffering when wronged or being self-restrained when attacked. Pastors are to be patient in their instruction as they bring the Word of God week after week. Even when it causes a reaction, they are to remain long-suffering and patient as they preach the truth to their congregations. Pastors must not be easily exasperated, like Moses who struck the rock in anger and was told by God, "You shall not bring this assembly into the land that I have given them" (Num. 20:8–13). Pastors must never take out their frustrations in the pulpit or display unwholesome and unrighteous anger in the pulpit. Rather, they are to be patient and loving toward those to whom they preach.

Always Giving Instruction

Paul commands that Timothy be "teaching" (2 Tim. 4:2). This carries the idea of instructing over and over again without losing heart or becoming exasperated. The word translated "instruction" (Greek *didachē*) refers to doctrinal teaching with theological precision. Pastors must be doctrinal teachers who bring forth theological accuracy from the text. Paul goes on to say in verse 3, "For the time is coming when people will not endure sound teaching." This encompasses the entirety of the church age, from the first to the second coming of Christ. Who are these people? They are those who sit under the pastor's preaching as unsaved church members. There are people sitting in the pews who will not endure sound doctrine and will instead desire softer messages without theological fiber. The Apostle Paul says they have "itching ears" (v. 3), wanting nothing more than to have their ears tickled and their egos massaged.

This is the reality of ministry. Pastors wrestle not with flesh and blood but against principalities, powers, and spiritual wickedness in the heavenly places in Christ. There are invisible forces of evil at work through people who want to have their ears tickled. They will run off preacher after preacher from the church until they have one who will tell them what they want to hear. Thus, they will accumulate for themselves teachers in accordance with their own desires and fire the ones who do not appeal to those desires. Paul instructs young Timothy that the opposition he will receive—and every true preacher will receive this opposition—will be great. Yet he must not cave in to the demands of carnal people or give them what they want to hear. Instead, he must stand up and be courageous and strong in the grace of the Lord Jesus Christ.

Being Sober-Minded

Paul goes on to speak of those who "will turn away from listening to the truth and wander off into myths" (2 Tim. 4:4). These people will sit in church, and as the Word is being exposited and application is being brought to their minds and hearts, they will turn away their ears and will turn aside to myths. They will listen to the falsehoods that are propounded by preachers who abuse the Word of God and extract from the Scripture meanings that are not in the text itself.

In response to all of this, Paul gives his fifth command to Timothy in verse 5: "As for you, always be sober-minded." This fifth imperative verb tells Timothy how he must preach. Timothy must be clearly different from these other preachers. He is not to be like the ear-ticklers who go from congregation to congregation and accumulate a following. This word "sober" literally means to be "free from intoxication." The preacher must be level-headed and unaffected by those who would seduce him into toning down his message. He must not become intoxicated by their attempts to control him or compromise the Word that he is to bring to the people.

Enduring Hardship in Preaching

Sixth, Paul commands, "endure suffering" (2 Tim. 4:5). Why would he say that? Because the more a pastor preaches the Word, the more hardship will come. The Bible is a sharp two-edged sword, a dangerous Book to unsheathe with all of its probing truths. As the pastor stands up to preach the Word, he becomes like a lightning rod in the storm. He is on the front lines of the battle—the most exposed, the most visible, and the most vocal—and he will receive the greatest hardship. In the midst of this, Paul says, "Endure it. Endure hardship. Persevere in your preaching." Pastors must preach the truth, the whole truth, and nothing but the truth.

Evangelizing the Church

Seventh, Paul instructs Timothy, "Do the work of an evangelist" (2 Tim. 4:5). The implication is that Timothy will be preaching to many who are unregenerate. They are spiritually blind and spiritually deaf, and this should stir the compassion of the pastor. Pastors should not become upset with unbelievers because they cannot see but should instead extend an arm to help them with kindness and patience. Only those who are lost can be evangelized, and as pastors preach the Word of God, they must remember the state in which the unconverted live. Pastors are describing a sunset to a blind man or a Beethoven symphony to a deaf man. The unbeliever cannot see or hear until the great day of God's power, when He opens his eyes and ears. But in the meantime, pastors are to be patient and bring much instruction as they do the work of an evangelist.

The greatest evangelistic work the pastor will ever do begins in his own congregation. The greatest mission field for the church is always its own members. Jesus said to the most religious crowd who has ever lived on the face of the earth, "Enter by the narrow gate. For the gate is wide and the way is easy that leads to destruction, and those who enter by it are many. For the gate is narrow and the way is hard that leads to life, and those who find it are few" (Matt. 7:13–14). Jesus went on to say, "Not everyone who says to me, 'Lord, Lord,' will enter the kingdom of heaven, but the one who does the will of my Father who is in heaven. On that day, many will say to me, 'Lord, Lord, did we not prophesy in your name, and cast out demons in your name, and do many mighty works in your name?' And then will I declare to them, 'I never knew you; depart from me, you workers of lawlessness'" (vv. 21–23). This is what Jesus had to say to the leaders of the most religious generation of His day, knowing many were lost and that He had to do the work of an evangelist.

Fulfilling Your Ministry

Eighth, Paul commands Timothy, "fulfill your ministry" (2 Tim. 4:5). Literally, the idea is to "fill it full." Timothy was to leave no truth untaught, no sin unexposed, no text unaddressed, and no invitation unissued. Likewise, pastors must discharge all the duties of their pastoral ministry, and at the heart of this ministry is the mandate to preach the Word and to preach all of the Word. They must strive to leave nothing unsaid, to be faithful to the very end, and to discharge their duties as men of God.

This is the call to expository preaching. The pastor extracts the true interpretation from the text, crafts the sermon, and steps into the pulpit before God and man to expound the unsearchable riches of Christ. He must plumb the depths of Scripture and ascend to the heights of heaven as he proclaims the message to all with much patience. This sharp two-edged sword will comfort the afflicted and afflict the comfortable, uproot and plant, lift up and bring down. The preaching of the Word of God will bring both salvation and damnation, both justification and judgment.

Now Is the Time

Many years ago, when I was a younger man, I heard John MacArthur preach a sermon in which he said, "Now is the time for the strongest men to preach the strongest message in the context

of the strongest ministry."[7] These words reached out ac
pews and laid hold of my heart. In this moment of tru
church needs pastors who will stand up and say, "God, I
one of those strongest men. I will not water down this
I will not compromise its message. I will bring an und
message. I will preach the strongest message."

By God's grace, may we see a new reformation. May
pastors be as icebreaker ships going out ahead and plowin
the hard ice, in order that many other ships may come in be
them and find safe passage. May all of God's shepherds dev
themselves to this heavenly calling to preach the Word for
glory of God and the good of His chosen people.

7. Justin Taylor, "A Conversation with John Piper and John Mac/
Desiring God, September 28, 2007, accessed October 8, 2017, http:
.desiringgod.org/interviews/a-conversation-with-john-piper-and-john-maca

10

A TRUTH-LED LIFE

The Reign of Truth in a Believer's Walk

The postmodern world in which we live is marked by its extreme denial of any authoritative truth. As believers, we must stand squarely upon the Word of God as we witness the rejection of truth, whether in the world or in the church. We must pursue the truth in our lives through a life of commitment to Jesus Christ. Throughout the centuries, believers have gained strength from the many godly examples of their historical predecessors. As we consider what a life of allegiance to Christ looks like, I want us to consider the example of the noted Scottish pastor Robert Murray M'Cheyne.

M'Cheyne's conversion to Jesus Christ came through personal tragedy. At age eighteen, he experienced the trauma of watching his older brother die. M'Cheyne was deeply impacted by the strong faith of his brother and the supernatural peace with which he faced death, and it led him to commit his life to

Jesus Christ. His conversion launched him into a life of ministry that would last only eleven years. M'Cheyne would himself die at the early age of twenty-nine. Though brief in years, his life was rich in depth.

A sickly young man, M'Cheyne was advised by his doctors to relocate to another climate in an effort to regain his health. So he sailed from Scotland to Europe and traveled to Israel in order to avail himself of the arid climate in the Middle East. Though instructed to rest, M'Cheyne spent his time in Israel evangelizing the Jews and preaching the gospel of the Lord Jesus Christ. He pushed himself to the very brink of exhaustion for the cause of the gospel. He recovered to some extent, returned to Scotland, and resumed his pastorate. A short time thereafter, M'Cheyne passed away.

Living Closer to Christ

Before his death, this young Scottish preacher wrote in his journal, "Set not your heart on the flowers of this world, for they all have a canker in them. Prize the rose of Sharon more than all, for He changes not. Live nearer to Christ than anyone else so that when they are taken from you, you may have Him to lean on still."[1] M'Cheyne lived with abandon; he held nothing back, investing his entire life with supreme devotion for the kingdom of God. Though he had only eleven years to live for Christ, the effect of this one life that was wholeheartedly committed to the

1. Robert Murray M'Cheyne, *Sermons* (New York: Robert Carter, 1848), 314.

Savior was such as though he lived eleven lifetimes. He was a mighty instrument in the hand of God, used to bring seasons of revival in the Church of Scotland.

The example of M'Cheyne should challenge each one of us to live with full commitment to Jesus Christ. As iron sharpens iron, so this fiery Scot should motivate our souls to live with greater abandon for the sake of Christ. What do you live for? What consumes and preoccupies you? What dominates your thoughts, ambitions, dreams, and aspirations? It is better to die at age twenty-nine and be radically committed to Jesus Christ than to live to be seventy or eighty years in passive mediocrity toward Him. The reign of truth in a believer's life is exemplified in the completely committed life of M'Cheyne. All who embrace the truth must pursue this decisive dedication as well, endeavoring to make every moment count for time and eternity.

One passage in the Bible that should inspire us to live in such a manner is Romans 12:1–2. This critically important text stands in a pivotal position in this epistle that is regarded as the most definitive doctrinal explanation of the gospel. After laying a theological foundation in the first eleven chapters of Romans, the Apostle Paul moves to its application. Here is how the gospel is to be lived on a daily basis. These two verses are the launching point for this new section on the reign of truth in our growing in grace.

Motivated by Divine Mercies

In discussing the practical aspect of living the Christian life, Romans 12:1 implores, "I appeal to you therefore, brothers, by the mercies of God. . . ." The greatest motivation for living for the Lord Jesus Christ is remembering the fullness of the saving mercies of God. This is a strong word of exhortation from the Apostle Paul issued to all believers. He is not encouraging his listeners with his personal persuasion to live for Christ. The motivation for following Jesus Christ, and thus the basis of Paul's appeal, is the mercies of God. This refers to the entirety of the saving grace of God wrought in eternal salvation that is described in the first eleven chapters of the book of Romans.

These preceding chapters in Romans make it clear that all mankind lies under the wrath of God (1:18). We have fallen short of the glory of God (3:23), we do not seek God (3:11–12), and we are entrenched in our sin (3:9). Yet consider what God has done for wretched sinners. God has justified us freely by His grace (3:24), giving us peace with Him (5:1). He "shows his love for us in that while we were still sinners, Christ died for us" (Rom. 5:8). God chose us in eternity past and predestined us for glory (8:29–30). Nothing will ever separate us from the love of God, which is in Christ Jesus our Lord (8:38–39). Once slaves of sin and ungodliness, we have been redeemed (3:24), set free, and resurrected to new life in Christ (6:4, 9). Consider what we have become: we are children of God, heirs of God, and joint-heirs with Christ (8:17). For those who are called according to His purpose, God is taking every circumstance, every trial, and every event, both great and small, and orchestrating it for His glory and our good (8:28).

These truths of our salvation are only a brief overview of what God has done to redeem us by His mercies. This should motivate us and compel us to live with full devotion to Jesus Christ. Do you understand what God has done for you in Christ? Are you truly motivated by the mercies of God to live in complete dedication for Him? The realization of what God has done for us in Christ Jesus should overwhelm us like a spiritual tsunami, flooding our souls, overwhelming us, and producing the motivation to do what He calls us to do.

Presenting Your Body

This motivation by the mercies of God should result in the presentation of our lives to Him. Paul writes, "present your bodies as a living and holy sacrifice, holy and acceptable to God" (Rom. 12:1). Here the Apostle calls for the decisive commitment of our whole lives as a living sacrifice to God. This is not a call to salvation, for that reality had already occurred in the lives of the believers in Rome. Rather, Paul is calling them to live their spiritual lives in a particular manner—as living sacrifices. This pictures the Old Testament sacrificial system, in which a priest would slay an animal, place it upon the altar, and offer it up to God as a sweet-smelling aroma that ascended upward to His throne. This sacrifice was a symbolic foreshadowing of the Lord Jesus Christ, our Great High Priest, who offered up Himself as the ultimate sacrificial Lamb to atone for our sins.

The death of Christ was the end of the ceremonial law and the sacrificial system. When He died, the veil of the temple was torn in two, from top to bottom (Matt. 27:51). This symbolized the access that every believer has to come to God directly through

Jesus Christ. Every believer is now a priest who may come boldly before the throne of grace. As priests, we do not bring a sacrificial lamb to God. Instead, we are to bring the sacrifice of our lives to God.

Giving God Everything

As worshipers, we are to give to God every part of our bodies. Nothing must be held back. We are to give Him our minds, including our thoughts, beliefs, dreams, and ambitions. We are to give Him our eyes—what we see, look upon, and focus upon. We are to give Him our ears—what we hear and listen to throughout the day. We are to give Him our mouths—what we say and what we teach. We are to give Him our hands—what we do and what we lay hold of. We are to give Him our feet—where we go and what we pursue. This is God's design for all believers. This is not reserved for the so-called spiritual elites, but for every true believer.

This kind of sacrificial life given to God requires that we must be continually coming before His throne of grace and presenting all that we are, all that we have, and all that we do and say, to all that He is. We must live our lives as though we are always on the altar before God. We must recognize that our life is no longer our own, but belongs to God.

Living Sacrifices to God

In the Old Testament, sacrifices were to be slain before they could be presented to God. Dead sacrifices were the requirement to please Him. But in the New Testament, we are instructed to present a living sacrifice to God. Meaning, we are to live for God and the things of His kingdom. This is the very purpose for which we have been redeemed. We are never more alive than when we are truly living for God. Any lesser life is a mere empty, hollow existence. The only way to experience the abundant life that Jesus came to give is to be a living sacrifice offered up to God.

Moreover, the Apostle Paul challenges the believers to be a "sacrifice" that is "holy," that is, set apart from the things of this world and totally given to God. This is the only sacrifice that is "acceptable to God" (Rom. 12:1). An unholy sacrifice is unacceptable to God. The book of Malachi depicts a half-hearted approach to God when the priests brought defective sacrifices to Him. They brought the blind, lame, and diseased animals to give to God. They kept for themselves the healthiest of the flock in order to sell them in the marketplace and line their pockets with money. God said they were to bring Him the very best they had to give (Mal. 1:6–14).

That is what Paul is calling for from us in this verse. We must give to God the best of our lives. Give Him the best hours of your day. Give Him the firstfruits of what He puts into your hands. Give God the very best that you have to offer Him, which, in reality, is the entirety of your life. That is the only presentation that is acceptable to God. The only way to live the Christian life in a manner acceptable to God is to be completely surrendered and radically committed to Jesus Christ. This is the kind of sacrifice that pleases Him. If you please God, it does not matter whom you displease, and if you displease God, it does not matter whom you please.

Is your life presented to God in this way? Does your practice match your position? Paul is saying that none of us is free to pursue our own agendas, plans, dreams, and aspirations. We only have one agenda in life, namely, to present our entire bodies on the altar as a living and holy sacrifice to God.

Spiritual Worship

Such a presentation of our lives to God is our "spiritual worship" (Rom. 12:1). This word "spiritual" (*logikos*) comes into our English language as *logic* or *logical* or *logarithms*. Paul is saying that this is the most rational or logical way to live based upon what God has done for believers in Christ. To live for the world, ourselves, or someone else is totally irrational. Based upon what Christ has done for us, the only reasonable way to live is for God. It is illogical and unreasonable to live for anyone or anything other than our Father who has shown us such mercy.

When the saving grace of God bestowed upon us is considered, it far outweighs any sacrifice that we make for Him. His commitment to us far outshines any persecution, opposition, and resistance that we would face for Him. We gain far more in Christ than we are called upon to give up for Him. We must live in this calculated manner, realizing that the gains we receive in Christ far exceed whatever losses we might experience in this world. In the spiritual ledger, the assets in Christ far outweigh the liabilities in following Him.

The noted Bible teacher James Montgomery Boice noted five ways to make this calculation.[2] First, consider what God has already done for you, especially all of the assets that you possess by His grace. Second, note what God is doing for you this very moment. Third, remember that it is God's will for you to live this way. Fourth, consider that God is worthy of your total sacrifice, allegiance, and loyalty. Fifth, remember that only spiritual things will last. How illogical it is to live for the temporal, passing things of this world. It is wasting, squandering, and throwing away your life to live for the things of this passing world.

Boice went on to assert that, spiritually, the most intelligent decision we will ever make is to completely give ourselves to Jesus Christ. We must not waste our lives like water being poured into the desert sand. We must not live for things that have no eternal significance. Instead, if we are to wisely invest our lives for the kingdom of God, we must present our bodies as living and holy sacrifices to God.

Insulated from the World

Paul has more to say, maintaining that believers must remain insulated from the world. He writes, "Do not be conformed to this world" (Rom. 12:2). Insulation from the world differs greatly from isolation. Too many Christians want to withdraw from the world and be completely disconnected from

2. James Montgomery Boice, *Renewing Your Mind in a Mindless World: Learning to Think and Act Biblically* (Grand Rapids, Mich.: Kregel, 2001), 65–70.

the world's system. However, we are to be in the world, but not of it. We are to advance into this world in order to reach people with the gospel of Jesus Christ. We must not become separated from those who need to hear the saving truth of Jesus Christ.

When Paul says that believers must not be conformed to this world, this clearly assumes that we will be in the world. This presupposes that we are penetrating the world of unbelievers, not retreating into our spiritual enclaves. We are to live in the very midst of this world. As we do, the challenge is to not become conformed to it. The word "conformed" means "to be squeezed into a mold." Believers must not be pressed into the values and pursuits of this world. "Do not be conformed" is an imperative verb, meaning this is a command. As we live in the world and engage with it, we are not to be compressed into its mold. We must be on guard against having our words, attitudes, and actions be influenced by the world system that surrounds us.

Resisting the World System

When Paul refers to the "world," he is addressing this present evil age (Rom. 12:2). It represents the world's system that is dominated by Satan. This system is anti-God, anti-Christ, and anti-truth. The mind-set of the world is worldly thinking, which views life as if all things are for the glory of man. The Apostle is emphatic that we must not buy into this false system with its selfish values, secular perspectives, and humanistic philosophies.

As Psalm 1:1 teaches, "Blessed is the man who walks not in the counsel of the wicked, nor stands in the way of sinners, nor sits in the seat of scoffers." Believers are to turn a deaf ear to the worldly ideologies, secular worldviews, and godless thinking that permeate the world in which we live.

Paul is saying that we must not give in to the world or let our guards down, because the world is never idle. Either we are influencing the world, or the world is influencing us. Either the world is the mission field or we are the mission field. The devil never sleeps. The forces of hell are aggressive, and we are subject to the relentless temptations, snares, and schemes of the evil one. We must insulate ourselves from the love of the world in order to protect ourselves in this battle. We must determine the things upon which we should never set our eyes. There is certain counsel to which we must not listen. There are certain practices in which we must never engage. We must be on guard and engaged in this pursuit.

Are you becoming more like the world, or is the world becoming more influenced by Christ as a result of your life?

Renewing the Mind

Living for Jesus Christ involves not only being insulated from the world but requires that we be transformed from the inside out. Paul maintains that we must "be transformed by the renewal of [our] mind[s]" (Rom. 12:2). This challenge refers to the radical change of our thinking that must occur if we are to be conformed into the likeness of Jesus Christ. The word translated "renew" (Greek *metamorphoō*) comes into the English language as *metamorphosis*. The Greek word means "to change into another form, to transfigure." This word was used to speak of the transfiguration of Christ when He was on the mountain with His three disciples (Matt. 17:2). This renewal speaks not of a mere superficial, external change, but the inward, spiritual progress in sanctification that transforms us from the inside out.

Please note the emphasis that Paul puts upon the importance of the believer's mind. The mind must first be transformed if the believer's life is to be transformed. The "mind" (Greek *nous*) refers to one's capacity to think, reason, understand, perceive, and judge. It includes the intellectual faculty of perceiving divine things. The mind controls the affections, and the affections control the will. This means that what comes into the mind has an effect on the heart. In turn, it is the heart that governs, steers, and directs the steps that a person chooses to take in life.

The mind that is being renewed by the Word of God will lead to a life that honors God. Conversely, the mind that is filled with the filth and depravity of this world will lead along a totally different path. Believers must be inwardly transformed if they are to become like Christ. The battle for the Christian mind is the battle for the Christian life. We must view life with the mind of Christ if we are to grow in grace. We must have God-given wisdom, discernment, and insight if we are to glorify God. The reign of the truth shapes our inner person and drives the entire course of our lives.

Discerning God's Will

What is the outcome of a life lived in complete commitment to the cause of Christ? What would it look like to give up living for temporal things that are superficial and peripheral? What would be the result of vowing to live for eternity and the things that matter most in God's kingdom? Paul does not leave us in suspense. He proceeds to tell us the result.

Paul concludes these two important verses by saying "that by testing you may discern what is the will of God" (Rom. 12:2). The word translated "discern" (Greek *dokimazō*) means "to test, examine, prove, scrutinize to see whether a thing is genuine or not." It means to recognize something as authentic after a careful examination. The word was used for the testing of a metal by putting it into a fiery furnace in order to discover if it was a precious metal or a base metal. The idea was to come to know something by personal experience. Paul is using the word to refer to a process that is more than knowing mere head knowledge. As the mind is renewed, believers will make a spiritual discovery of the will of God for their own lives.

This discovery involves a differentiation not merely between good and evil in a person's life. Rather, this involves distinguishing between what is good, better, and best. Paul describes this will of God as "good and acceptable and perfect" (v. 2). The will of God is first of all "good" (Greek *agathos*), meaning it is "pleasant, agreeable, joyful, excellent, upright." The will of God is not like taking bad medicine in order to get well. Rather, it is the very best path that leads to the greatest blessings and satisfaction that we could ever know. It is "good," meaning that it leads to our spiritual and moral good, for our own good and God's glory. In other words, we experience second best and a lesser good when we do not live this way.

This path in life is also "acceptable" (Greek *evarestos*), meaning "well-pleasing, agreeable." Rather than being dragged into obedience against our wills, we will find great pleasure as we experience the fullness of doing God's will and His work. This way is "perfect" (Greek *teleios*), meaning "complete, ripe, lacking nothing." If we had a thousand lifetimes to try to re-chart the course of our lives for the best direction, we could never improve upon it one iota, because what God has already chosen for our lives is absolutely perfect. Any path we might conceive for ourselves would be less than perfect, but God's chosen path for us is complete, whole, and lacking in nothing. It is the very best life we could ever live or experience.

Surrendering to God

Every one of us must come to the place where we humble ourselves before God and commit ourselves afresh to live for Him. We must be fully surrendered to Him, striving for what is of eternal significance. We must come to God in lowly humility of mind and present our bodies as a priest would sacrifice an animal on the altar. We must offer to God our minds, our thoughts, our time, our strengths, and our gifts, as each passing day narrows the gap between our earthly lives and our eternal lives. We give Him our present and our future, everything that we have and everything we will ever be.

The reign of truth in our lives results in a life completely committed to Christ, as a living sacrifice would be placed upon the altar. We came into the kingdom of God by surrendering our lives to the lordship of Christ. We must daily acknowledge our original commitment to live under His supreme authority. C.T. Studd wrote, "Only one life, 'twill soon will be passed; only what's done for Christ will last."[3] We must choose to give our lives entirely to Christ and follow Him wherever He goes. We must be renewing this commitment daily, and when we see the Lord Jesus in glory, you and I will have no regrets for a life lived in the truth of God.

3. The publication of the poem is unknown. Cited in Malcolm Gill, *Knowing Who You Are: Eight Surprising Images of Christian Identity* (Eugene, Ore.: Wipf & Stock, 2015), 22.

11

TRUTH-IGNITED WORSHIP

The Reign of Truth in the Highest Worship

A new way of doing church has emerged in recent years. This new approach is virtually unprecedented in the history of the church and takes its cues from the world. The goal seems to be to make the gathering of the church on Sunday morning look as much like the world as possible. This radical paradigm shift is designed to attract the world by creating an atmosphere that mirrors the world in almost every respect. The ambiance of the worship service has been reconfigured in order to make an unconverted person feel as comfortable as possible.

This new way changes worship into an experience designed to be casual and trendy. Rather than embracing timeless transcendence, churches seek what is cool and cutting-edge. The emphasis is no longer upon reverence, but upon being relaxed. The music evokes either the nonchalant mood of a local Starbucks on one hand, or a fan-frenzied, decibel-blasting music concert on the other. These changes in worship are the necessary result of changes in preaching. No longer is expositional preaching the goal. Instead, the preacher wants to be trendy, chatty, brief, and felt-need oriented. He desires to be more therapeutic than theological.

On a typical Sunday morning in many churches, the infinite has been replaced with the informal, exposition has been replaced with entertainment, and a vertical focus has been replaced with a horizontal emphasis. The transcendent has given way to the trendy and trivial, doctrine has been replaced with drama, and theology has been eclipsed by theatrics. The truth of God is being exchanged for the ways of the world. All of these replacements are oriented toward removing the barriers between the church and the world in order to make the church more attractive to unbelievers. Yet this approach of becoming like the world in order to win the world is incongruous. By looking at the world in order to fashion the worship service, the church is looking in the wrong direction. The church needs to look to heaven, where the purest worship is being given to God. God Himself has designed the worship service in heaven to bring Him the greatest glory. We would do well to mirror the worship in heaven during our time here upon the earth.

In his book *A Taste of Heaven*, R.C. Sproul argues convincingly that all worship on the earth should be anticipatory of heaven and should be a foretaste of heaven. Sproul then asks, "If God Himself were to design worship, what would it look like?"[1] Another way to phrase the question might be this: What

---

1. R.C. Sproul, *A Taste of Heaven: Worship in the Light of Eternity* (Orlando, Fla.: Reformation Trust, 2006), 15.

does the reign of truth look like when it comes to worship? Of course, the answer to this question is found in the Word of God.

Revelation 4 contains the perfect worship service. It is designed by God Himself. Here we learn the elements of truth in worship as the Apostle John relays his experience. What does he see? What does he hear? What does he feel? Revelation 4 contains a rare glimpse into the throne room of heaven and the rightful praise being given to God. The Apostle John has been caught up in his spirit into the heights of heaven and is given a vision of the heavenly scene. What he sees is absolutely breathtaking.

This distinctly theocentric passage contains five marks of heavenly worship. All worship services of the church should bear these divine distinctives.

A High View of God

First, the reign of truth in worship begins with God Himself. It starts with a high view of God in the heights of heaven.

As John stepped into heaven, he entered a worship service that was already in progress. This scene was primarily designed to exalt and magnify God Himself. John was immediately struck by the fact that he was in another world, as it was unlike anything he had experienced. As John entered heaven, what first captured his attention? It was not who was or was not there. Nor was it the streets of gold or the gates of pearl. The first reality that struck John and dominated his attention was the throne of God.

This throne represents the absolute sovereignty of Almighty God. It towers over all of human history. This throne indicates the reign of God over every human life and eternal destiny. It was this throne that immediately grabbed John's attention. Instantly, he was overwhelmed by an awareness of the supreme authority of God over all the universe. This was the dominant theme of this worship service in heaven.

Towering over All

John needed to be reminded of the reign of God. As the last living Apostle, he was suffering exile on the island of Patmos and enduring persecution. From his vantage point, it seemed as though Caesar of Rome was in control during the darkest hour of the early church. From John's earthly perspective, it looked as though the enemies of the gospel were triumphing and that the devils of hell were reigning. But upon stepping into this worship service, John experienced an immediate change of perspective. He saw that it was not Caesar who is in charge of the world. Neither do Satan, man, circumstances, or blind chance rule the day. Rather, as John saw, the One who sits on the throne in heaven presides over all.

John further notes of the throne that it was "standing" in heaven. This indicates that the throne is fixed, permanent, and unshakable. This throne is unaltered, unchanged, and unswayed by human leaders. The caesars on the throne of Rome come and go, but this heavenly throne remains standing. Human history ebbs and flows, but this throne remains towering over the entire universe.

In Revelation 4, everything in heaven is viewed in its relationship to the throne: God is *on* the throne (v. 2), the elders are *around* the throne (v. 4), thunder and lightning proceed *from* the throne (v. 5), the sea of glass is *below* the throne (v. 6), all glory goes *to* the One on the throne (v. 9), and the elders fall *before* the One on the throne (v. 10). Everything in heaven is measured by its proximity to the throne. Whether it is on, around, from, below, or next to the throne, the throne is the epicenter of all that is there, and it is God who is upon it.

This Dominating Throne

John also records that this throne is occupied. It is not a vacant or empty throne, but there is One seated upon this throne. The Apostle sees that God has permanently assumed His position upon the throne. This Sovereign will never be impeached or removed from office. The Apostle sees that God is actively presiding, ruling, and reigning over history. He is governing every moment throughout the eternities to come. This truth dominates the vision that John receives. The Apostle does not name who is upon the throne; he does not need to. It is obvious who it is. The occupier of the throne is none other than the sovereign of heaven and earth—the One who speaks and it is done, the One who acts and it holds fast, the One who wills and it is completed. This enthroned ruler is God Himself.

From this throne shines the radiant glory of God that is bursting forth. John compares the One upon the throne to a jasper stone—crystal clear in His purity, holiness, and glory.

Around the throne John sees a rainbow with the appearance of an emerald, which no doubt represents God's covenant faithfulness to His people. The beauty of these valuable stones represents something of the perfect attributes, character, glory, and majesty of Almighty God. As John stares into this throne room, he speaks of the royal majesty of God, whose stately splendor offers a vivid display of His awesome glory.

Redeemed of the Ages

Around the throne are twenty-four thrones, which are lesser thrones under the domination and direction of the ultimate throne of God. These subordinate thrones possess a delegated authority from God to rule and reign with Him. Upon these thrones are the twenty-four elders, representing the redeemed of the saints from all of the ages. They are "clothed in white garments" (Rev. 4:4), representing the perfect righteousness of Christ imputed to them in justification. They stand faultless and blameless before the very throne of God, not due to their own works, but because of the perfect righteousness of Him who lived a perfect life and bore their sins upon Calvary's cross. The "golden crowns on their heads" (v. 4) are the victors' crowns, awarded to those who have persevered in life and ministry. There is a note of victory in this worship service, as those who share in the righteousness of Christ share in His glorious exaltation. There is no sense of defeat in this worship service, but only the supreme and ruling will of God over all of humanity.

At the forefront of a God-centered worship service is a preoccupation with the supreme sovereignty of God. What people should sense as they enter a worship service is that they have left the world behind and stepped into the world above. They should realize that they have stepped into the presence of the King of heaven. An overriding sense of the towering transcendence of God should be conveyed to worshipers. When people enter a church worship service, they should not be struck by the horizontal but by the vertical. They should not be struck by the church's adaptability to the world, but rather struck by the church's identity with Almighty God, the One who is seated upon this throne, who is ruling and reigning over all of history.

As we step into the worship service, there must be a sense that we have left the realm where Satan, sin, and demons reign and have entered into the heavenly realm where God alone reigns. Contrarily, when man is the preoccupation, when the world is the pattern, and when we have a low ceiling in the ministry of the Word of God, then the worship of God is equally low. Do you sense this high and towering view of God as you walk into a worship service? When you are alone with God and come before Him with an open Bible, what do you experience? Do you sense that you are entering into the throne room of God through Christ? Do you perceive that you now have an audience with the King of kings? The first distinctive of this heavenly worship service is a high view of God, and we cannot have too high a view of God.

Deep Fear of God

Second, a God-centered worship service should be marked by a deep fear of God. A high view of God should promote a deep reverence for God. This heavenly worship service is marked by awe-struck worshipers. John is gripped with the sobering reality of entering into the presence of Almighty God. Out of the throne come "flashes of lightning, and rumbling and peals of thunder" (Rom. 4:5). There is nothing soft and gentle about this scene, as the thundering fiery presence of God captures John's attention.

The tone of this heavenly scene is dominant, commanding, compelling, and intended to reflect the majestic supremacy of God. No one in this setting is being casual with God. No one is trying to be cool—not with lightning and thunder proceeding from the throne of God. This gathering storm in heaven is intended to evoke a healthy, reverential awe and holy fear of Him. How different this is from so many worship services today, where it seems that the goal is to do everything possible to remove the fear of God. In contemporary services, the intent is to create a relaxed, informal feel. However, the worship service in heaven strikes a totally different mood, one marked by sobriety and seriousness from those in attendance. The presence of God is attention grabbing, soul arresting, and heart gripping. It is not toned down to make the saints feel comfortable. Rather, it is intended to convey the awesomeness of God that leaves the worshipers trembling.

No Casual Worship

The fear of God is an essential component of any true worship of God. Proverbs 1:7 says, "The fear of the LORD is the beginning of knowledge." From this, we may conclude that the fear of God is also the beginning of worship. Psalm 2:11 says, "Serve the LORD with fear, and rejoice with trembling." Our service of God must include fear with trembling before we can rejoice in Him. Psalm 5:7 says, "I will bow down toward your holy temple in the fear of you." Here it is clear that we must take God seriously in worship. We must realize that we are living on His earth, breathing His air, drinking His water, and living within the parameters that He has established. This realization should produce deep fear and reverence for God.

Tragically, we seem to have lost this sense of the fear of God in church. Do you see yourself growing in the fear of God in the worship at the church where you attend? Solomon wrote, "Fear God and keep his commandments, for this is the whole duty of man" (Eccl. 12:13). Thus, the fear of God is not merely the beginning of wisdom, but also the end of wisdom and everything in between. We should be growing in our reverential respect and honor for God as we grow in His grace.

Still Separated from God

Third, this heavenly worship service revealed a distinct separation from God. Even in heaven, God remains God, and the glorified saints remain but glorified creatures. The vast expanse of "a sea of glass, like crystal" (Rev. 4:6) sets God apart from His creation.

We will be in the presence of God, as we rule and reign with Christ as joint heirs. Yet the vast sea of glass will still separate God from His creatures. In Revelation 21:23, we read that there is no more sun, as the bright shining glory of God Himself will illuminate the entire universe. As we stand in the presence of the Lord, He will shine brighter than ten thousand suns in the sky above. In our glorified bodies, perfectly adapted for our new heavenly home, we will be able to look upon His face in order to glorify Him.

Everything continues to be defined by the throne, as it stands as the epicenter of the universe. Around the throne are the "four living creatures" (Rev. 4:6), identified as cherubim in Ezekiel 10:15. These angelic beings serve as guardians of the glory of God. In Genesis 3:24, they were positioned at the entrance of the garden of Eden to keep Adam and Eve from returning. Two carved cherubim were placed in the Holy of Holies, symbolically representing their guardianship of God's holiness (1 Kings 6:23, 28). In fact, Satan was once the anointed cherub, that one who was closest to the throne of God (Ezek. 28:14, 16). Anyone who dared approach the throne in an attempted coup would have to pass through these cherubim.

Guarding the Throne

Though these angelic beings are real, their function is merely symbolic. In actuality, no one can remove God from His throne. They serve as a visual reminder that God is set apart, even from His glorified creatures, and cannot be approached carelessly. These creatures are "full of eyes in front and behind" (Rev. 4:6). That is, they are in constant vigil, looking and seeing in every direction. No one is allowed to approach the throne without their awareness. They are in a state of constant surveillance, always alert, always awake, maintaining a perpetual state of readiness. It is no small matter for glorified saints to approach this sovereign God, even in heaven.

John records, "The first living creature [is] like a lion" (v. 7), indicating he is strong in his service of God. "The second living creature [is] like an ox," sacrificial in its service of God. The third has "the face of a man," imbued with intelligence and reason in service to God. "The fourth living creature [is] like an eagle," swift to fly away to carry out God's bidding. Each of the creatures has "six wings" (v. 8). With two wings they cover their face, Isaiah wrote, as they are unable to gaze upon God's blinding glory without covering their eyes (Isa. 6:2). With two wings, they cover their feet, conveying a sense of their utter unworthiness to be in the presence of the Holy One. With two wings they fly, ready to soar across the universe to carry out the will of the One upon the throne. This certainly represents how the believer is to serve God. We are to be ready and strong in our commitment to serve Him, all the while with a sense of unworthiness to be in the service of such a majestic King.

Any power that we possess is but a delegated power that has come to us from God. It is through Him that we live and move and have our being, and all power and might belong to God alone. Nothing is impossible for Him, so no resistance can ever succeed against Him. His creative power spoke all things into existence out of nothing, and His sustaining power upholds all that He has made. His governing power providentially rules over all circumstances and events, His saving power rescues the chief of sinners, and His judging power damns those who fall short of His glory. As Psalm 115:3 asserts, "Our God is in the heavens; he does all that he pleases." Heaven is not a democracy but a theocracy. God is not trendy but transcendent, rising above time. He is God of eternity, from everlasting to everlasting.

Fervently Praising God

Fourth, the worship of God in heaven is also marked by constant praise for God. John records that the four living creatures day and night never cease to say, "Holy, holy, holy, is the Lord God Almighty, who was and is and is to come" (Rev. 4:8). These living creatures do not cease from this ongoing worship, continuously crying out day and night, "Holy, holy, holy." Holiness is the only divine attribute singled out in the worship of God, as it is the summation of all that God is. The heavenly choir is not singing "Love, love, love," though God is perfect love. They are not singing "Grace, grace, grace," though He is the God of all grace. Instead, they are lifting their voices and crying out, "Holy, holy, holy," which encompasses the entire being of God.

The holiness of God speaks of His complete separation from His creation. This chief attribute means that God is majestic and transcendent, high and lifted up, set apart from all evil. Holiness also means that God is absolutely perfect in His being, without any moral blemish or stain of sin. His ways, words, works, and judgments are perfect. In this angelic chorus, God's holiness is repeated three times—"holy, holy, holy"—to indicate holiness to the superlative degree. This threefold repetition signifies that He is holy, holier, and holiest. God is completely distinct from and above all other beings. He is utterly sinless and absolutely pure. This aspect of God is what is singled out in the worship above.

This fervent praise of God's holiness should mark every worship service upon the earth. Everything that does not pass through the paradigm of the holiness of God should be left at the front door. There is no place for triviality or frivolity before a holy God. There is no room for triteness in the presence of this thrice-holy God. There is no place for the secular ideologies of this world as we worship Him who is infinitely holy. The Bible declares, "There is none holy like the Lord" (1 Sam. 2:2). God alone is "majestic in holiness" (Ex. 15:11). He is "of purer eyes than to see evil and cannot look at wrong" (Hab. 1:13). He "sits on his holy throne" (Ps. 47:8), and He declares to Israel that "I am holy" (Lev. 11:44).

The chief preoccupation of this heavenly worship service is God. Every eye is riveted upon Him throughout this scene. Every voice is raised toward Him. The living creatures "give glory and honor and thanks to him who is seated on the throne, who lives forever and ever" (Rev. 4:9). These angelic beings are ascribing "glory" to Him who alone is worthy of this fervent praise. Worshipers give to God the "honor"—the rightful recognition—that belongs to Him alone. And they give God "thanks" because they recognize that every blessing in their lives has proceeded from Him. Worshipers are primarily givers to God, rendering to Him glory, honor, and thanks. They never come with a self-preoccupation for what they can get out of Him but with the selfless intent to give God the praise He alone deserves.

Falling Down before God

Fifth, in response to this glorious sight, all creatures in the presence of God fall down before Him in humble submission. John records, "The twenty-four elders fall down before him" (Rev. 4:10) as they collapse before His throne again and again. Repeatedly in the book of Revelation, the elders prostrate themselves before God (Rev. 4:10; 5:8, 14; 7:11; 11:16; 19:4). They worship "him who lives forever and ever. They cast their crowns before the throne" (4:10). This act of casting their crowns back before the throne of God signifies that all things are from Him, and through Him, and now to Him (Rom. 11:36).

The elders "cast their crowns before the throne" (Rev. 4:10) because they rightly realize that all things in their earthly lives had been accomplished by the grace of God alone. God chose them in eternity past and predestined their eternal salvation. God sent His Son to die for them and gave His Spirit to convict them of sin, righteousness, and judgment. God caused their new birth when they were dead in trespasses and sins and empowered them for every good work. God safely brought them all the way home to glory before His throne of grace. They cannot keep these crowns upon their heads, for such recognition belongs to God alone. With a deeper awareness of His grace, the redeemed cast themselves and their crowns at His feet.

This enlarged realization of God in His glory provokes a towering anthem of praise to God. The heavenly worshipers cry out, "Worthy are you, our Lord and God, to receive glory and honor and power, for you created all things, and by your will they existed and were created" (v. 11). All of heaven resounds in praise to God as those around the throne come to greater awareness of His transcendent majesty. This worship declares the greatness of God, who alone deserves to receive all our praise and glory. Based on their understanding of God's awesomeness, they ascribe glory to His name. A distinction should be made between two aspects of God's glory: His intrinsic glory and His ascribed glory. God's intrinsic glory is all that He is, including the sum of His divine attributes, being, and perfections. No one can add to this intrinsic glory or diminish it. God is who He is, and He remains forever as He is, unchanging in His eternal perfections.

On the other hand, ascribed glory consists of the glory that the creature must give to God. The more we understand of His intrinsic glory, the more we will ascribe glory to Him. This is the worship that they are rendering to Him in heaven. As they see more of the infinite perfections of His holiness, those in the immediate presence of God give Him even greater worship and praise. The greater their vision of God, the greater their adoration of Him.

This worshiping throng declares, "You created all things, and by your will they existed and were created" (v. 11). This awe-inspiring God spoke everything into existence out of nothing. He stood in eternity past, declaring the end from the beginning, and called everything into being in both creation and providence. His sovereign will has caused all things to be created and governed by Him. In heaven, He receives ceaseless worship for all that He is and for all that He has done, is doing, and will do.

Heaven on Earth

This is the worship service that is taking place in heaven. If the church on earth is to respond to the reign of truth in heaven, we must pattern our earthly worship after this heavenly model. A.W. Tozer famously said, "The most important thing about your life is what comes into your mind when you think of God. That everything in your life is a subsequent effect of this one central knowledge of God."[2] It is our high view of God that leads to high worship and holy living. Making this same emphasis, John Calvin began his *Institutes of the Christian Religion* by emphasizing the knowledge of God and the knowledge of self. Calvin rightly understood that everything in our lives flows from our knowledge of God. Even our knowledge of self flows from the knowledge of God.

A high view of God will lead to awe-inspiring, transcendent worship and holiness-pursuing, godly living. But conversely, a low view of God will lead to low, trivial worship and low, worldly living. Our knowledge of God affects all that we are and all that we do. Tell me who you believe God is, and I will tell you much about the direction and devotion of your life. Therefore, the greatest thing that can happen in a worship service is the unveiling of the greatness, glory, and grandeur of God.

2. A.W. Tozer, *The Knowledge of the Holy* (New York: HarperCollins, 1961), 1.

Let us possess a high view of God that will always produce a deep fear of Him. Let us give resounding praise to Him, remembering that He is forever our God, and we are His people and the sheep of His pasture. The reign of truth demands the appropriate worship of God, and we must reject all attempts to inject worldly motives and methods into the worship of our Almighty God. Instead, let us model our worship after what is taking place in heaven around the throne of God. May we strive to worship Him on earth as He is being worshiped in heaven.

12

TRUTH AT THE JUDGMENT

The Reign of Truth in the Final Judgment

What happens to those who die while denying the truth of God in their lives? What will their rejection of the truth mean for them? Most people today do not want to think about the final judgment. For those who are young, death and eternity seem so far away. Yet if we would think seriously about eternity—heaven and hell—it would change the way we live today, and for many, it will change where they will spend eternity. Theologian and author R.C. Sproul notes, "Modern man is betting his eternal destiny that there is no final judgment."[1] This is a tragically fatal bet. The holiness and righteousness of God demand that He execute perfect justice on the final day. At the end of human history, God will judge the world, and His eternal purpose for redemptive history will, at last, be fulfilled.

1. Cited in Charles W. Colson and Ellen S. Vaughn, *The Body: Being Light in Darkness* (Dallas: Word, 1992), 165.

Looming on the horizon of eternity, there is coming a terrifying final day of judgment. This world is spinning through space on a collision course with this final day of reckoning. Known as the great white throne judgment, this climactic hour of reckoning before God is described in numerous places throughout Scripture. The book of Romans identifies it as "the day of wrath" (Rom. 2:5). Jude calls it "the judgment of the great day" (Jude 6). The Apostle Paul says that God "has fixed a day on which he will judge the world in righteousness" (Acts 17:31). This day is fast approaching—a final judgment day in which God will hold court, and all the world will stand trial before Him. In this final judgment, God will open the books and present His case. Every lost sinner will be judged, and God will announce His just verdict and condemn every unbeliever to hell.

This final courtroom scene is described with dramatic detail in Revelation 20:11–15. This is the highest court in heaven or on earth. It is the supreme court of the universe, and there is no higher court of appeal. Every lost sinner will be individually summoned to take his stand before the divine judgment bar, where every unbeliever will have his day in court before the Lord Jesus Christ. The evidence will be presented, and it will be an irrefutable case presented by God Himself. There will be no rebuttal offered, no defense rendered, and no sympathy extended. There will be no grace, no advocate to defend the sinner, and no miscarriage of justice. There will be no successful appeal by the guilty, and no parole from prison as an escape. There will only be perfect judgment. Let us now look carefully at this final judgment.

The Throne of Heaven Revealed

This last scene is described in only a few words, but how sober they are with the truth that must be heard. This is no imaginary scene, but rather a real day. The magnitude of this moment cannot be overstated. This is a day unalterably fixed on God's prophetic calendar, and mankind is moving irreversibly toward this final day. The reign of truth in the final judgment is clearly seen in this setting, as sinners will be summoned, their sins disclosed, and the sentence delivered.

As the Apostle John begins to describe the vision, he records, "Then I saw a great white throne" (Rev. 20:11). The setting of this momentous event is the very throne of Almighty God. The word "great" speaks of its awesome power, "white" speaks to its absolute purity, and "throne" speaks to its avenging purpose. John's eyes are riveted upon the stark reality of the terrifying scene as it is unveiled before his eyes. We want to consider what each of these three words indicates regarding the gravity of this final judgment.

This throne is described as "great," towering over every other throne in the universe. It possesses jurisdiction over the entire created order. It overrides every decision of any lower human court. It is great in its authority to render verdicts and great in its authority to execute its judgments. Its summons are irresistible, and its verdicts are final. It is the greatest courtroom in the world.

A Day of Inflexible Justice

This divine throne is further revealed as being "white." This indicates that it is a court of absolute holiness and inflexible justice. There will be no injustice or partiality shown by this throne. Every sinful deed will be entered into the courtroom as condemning evidence. The secrets of men's hearts will be exposed and presented exactly for what they were. There will be no exaggeration in this courtroom, as every piece of evidence for every sinful thought, motive, and deed will be presented exactly as it is. This holy Judge cannot be bribed. No mistrial can be declared. No legal loopholes will be found.

The word "throne" speaks of the purpose assigned. "Throne" indicates this is a judge's tribunal, thus, a seat of judgment. Here, every sin will be presented and judgment rendered. In this final judgment, sinners will be the objects of the righteous anger and fury of Almighty God. This last day is fast approaching, for it is necessary that the holiness, righteousness, and perfect justice of God be executed. Holy God cannot excuse wrongs committed; they must be judged. No sin can be overlooked in a moral universe under the government of righteous God.

The entire Bible has looked ahead to this final courtroom scene of divine judgment. Psalm 9:7–8 says, "But the LORD sits enthroned forever; he has established his throne for justice." Psalm 7:11–13 elaborates, "God is a righteous judge, and a God who feels indignation every day. If a man does not repent, God will whet his sword; he has bent and readied his bow; he has prepared for him his deadly weapons, making his arrows fiery shafts." Every one of these divine arrows of judgment are aimed at lost sinners—and God never misses His target.

The Judge of Heaven Identified

The One who sits upon this throne of judgment is none other than the Lord Jesus Christ Himself. He is revealed here not by name but rather by His activity in executing divine justice. He is the One who has been the primary focus of the book of Revelation. The Scripture elsewhere identifies this Judge as the Lord Jesus Christ. Jesus said Himself, "For the Father judges no one, but has given all judgment to the Son" (John 5:22). It will be before Jesus Christ that every lost person will stand. Peter announced, "He is the one appointed by God to be judge of the living and the dead" (Acts 10:42). Further, Paul declares, "On that day when, according to my gospel, God judges the secrets of men by Christ Jesus" (Rom. 2:16). He is seated, actively presiding in judgment. When an earthly judge is seated, it means that the court is in session. He is in session, ready to judge on this day. The Lamb of God shall become a Lion in that day. This Lion will crush His prey with His mighty jaws and consume them. The Lion of the tribe of Judah will rightfully capture and judge every unbeliever.

In this final day, every lost sinner will stand face-to-face with the Lord Jesus Christ. They will see Him with hair like snow and wool, His feet like burnished bronze, His eyes like a flame of fire, His voice like the roar of many waters, and His face shining like the sun (Rev. 1:14–16). His voice will drown out every excuse that would be offered to Him. His condemning verdict alone will be heard. This is the setting of the great white throne judgment, and we cannot conceive of a more terrifying scene than the one described here—to appear at the throne of the great judge of heaven and earth and receive perfect, inflexible justice.

When all the unsaved, guilty sinners see this terrifying Judge, they will do all they can to escape in absolute terror. Yet we read, "No place was found for them" (Rev. 20:11). This throne is inescapable and this judgment unavoidable. All godless men must appear before the Lord Jesus Christ, and they will have no place to hide in the final day. During their rebellious lives, they ignored, denied, blasphemed, and marginalized Christ. They played games with Him and cursed His name. They denied the reality of truth in the message of His cross until their dying day. All that remains for them is the retribution of truth in the final judgment.

The Sinners of History Summoned

This Judge possesses all authority and power to summon the guilty. He will merely issue the divine subpoena, and every unconverted sinner will be brought to appear before Him. "And I saw the dead, great and small, standing before the throne" (Rev. 20:12). He has no red tape with which to deal. He has no legalities with which to contend. The multitude before the throne will include all the unsaved dead since the beginning of time, summoned to appear in His heavenly courtroom. John saw the "great" standing here, a reference to the great men in history who lived with great influence over others. Here will stand Alexander the Great, Napoleon, Hitler, Stalin, and many other notorious rulers who sinned on a grand scale with the world as their stage.

These great men have summoned others to appear before them. But now, the table is turned. They are the ones summoned to give an account of themselves to the Judge of heaven and earth.

John witnessed the "small" standing there as well. These are the unknown individuals of history who were small in position, small in visibility, and small in influence during their earthly lives. They lived lives of obscurity, with little or no significance upon the populace. They were unknown men and anonymous women, who amounted to little in the grand scheme of the world. They simply drew their breath and drew their salary. These are our next-door neighbors, our colleagues at the office, and our classmates at school. They lived rather common lives, far removed from the public eye. But the Lord sees them, the Lord knows about them, and the Lord will summon them to appear before Him on the last day.

A Wide Host of People

When this divine summons is issued, the types of people that will stand at the great white throne will be varied. First, the out-and-out sinner will be there. This includes those who have sinned violently against God, who have broken His law with a high hand, and who, if they could, would spit in the face of the Lord Jesus Christ. This is the company of those who blaspheme God, despise the church, hate the Bible, and mock any form of morality. These have lived lives of open, shameless sin. To be sure, they will be brought to stand before the judge and have their day in court.

Second, the self-righteous will also stand in the judgment. This includes those who prided themselves in their goodness and morality. They believed that the gospel was for the thief, the prostitute, and the out-and-out sinner, but it was not for them. They thought that they were good enough by their own good works to commend themselves to God. They assumed that they were better than others and presumed that God would grade them on a curve and accept them. But the reality is, they have been weighed in the balances of divine justice and found wanting. They have sinned and fallen short of the glory of God. They, too, will be brought to stand in this last day.

Third, cult members from every false religion will also appear at the great white throne judgment. These are the ones who have followed the teaching of false religious leaders such as Muhammad, Buddha, Joseph Smith, and Sun Myung Moon, or any number of countless other false teachers. They have followed the damning lies and belief systems of these religious teachers. There are many roads leading to hell, but only one way to God. "There is a way that seems right to a man, but its end is the end of death" (Prov. 14:12).

Let us be clear that there is only one way of salvation, and that is through Jesus Christ. Jesus said, "I am the way, and the truth, and the life. No one comes to the Father except through me" (John 14:6). The Scripture says, "For there is one God, and there is one mediator between God and men, the man Christ Jesus, who gave himself as a ransom for all, which is the testimony given at the proper time" (1 Tim. 2:5–6). Peter proclaimed, "There is salvation in no one else, for there is no other name under heaven given among men by which we must be saved" (Acts 4:12). Every follower of any false religion will be summoned to stand before the Lord Jesus Christ at the great white throne judgment and will have no defense.

Procrastinators and Church Members

Fourth, those who procrastinated and intended to commit their life to Jesus Christ, but never did, will also appear on that day. This includes those individuals who knew that they were sinners and that Jesus Christ is the Son of God who is the Savior of sinners. They intended to be saved one day, but kept putting off this most important decision. One day, they reasoned, they would commit their life to Christ, but that day never came. One day after college, one day after getting married, one day after having children, one day after becoming settled in their career, then they would give their lives to Christ. But that day never came. Proverbs 27:1 says, "Do not boast about tomorrow, for you do not know what a day may bring." Because of this, the Bible urges all, saying, "Behold, now is the favorable time; behold, now is the day of salvation" (2 Cor. 6:2). Consequently, procrastinators who die without Christ will be summoned to stand before the great white throne.

Fifth, lost church members will also be summoned to appear before the great white throne. They grew up in the church, joined the church, married in the church, and were eulogized in the church at their funeral, but were never truly born again. They have their name on the church roll, but it was never written in the Lamb's

Book of Life. They profess Christ, but never possessed Him. They are attached to the church, but they were never attached to the Lord Jesus Christ. These are the ones who will say, "Lord, Lord, did we not prophesy in your name, and cast out demons in your name, and do many mighty works in your name?" And Jesus will say to them, "I never knew you; depart from me, you workers of lawlessness" (Matt. 7:22–23). These unconverted church members will be summoned to appear before this great white throne judgment because they refused to believe in Jesus Christ, who said, "Unless one is born again he cannot see the kingdom of God" (John 3:3).

The Dead Bodies Raised

Each unconverted sinner will be raised from the dead and brought to stand before Jesus Christ. Revelation 20:13 tells, "And the sea gave up the dead who were in it." In ancient times, the bodies of those who went down with the ship and perished at sea were considered irretrievable. Their bodies would sink into the depths of the sea, never to be seen again. Yet on this last day, Jesus Christ will raise the dead from the depths of the ocean. As the Lord Jesus Christ issues His summons from the great white throne, the sea itself will give up the dead that lie at the bottom of its depths.

Not only will the sea give up its dead, but "Death and Hades gave up the dead who were in them" (v. 13). "Death and Hades" refers to the grave, those places on dry land where dead bodies lie buried. On this last day, their decayed corpses will be raised up and reunited with their tormented souls to have their official day in court. Jesus said, "Do not marvel at this; for an hour is coming, when all who are in the tombs will hear his voice and come out, . . . those who have done evil to the resurrection of judgment" (John 5:28–29). There they will stand, before this fearsome and awesome Judge on that last day.

Opened Books in Heaven

In this divine judgment, the sins of those without Christ will be disclosed. In the middle of Revelation 20:12, we read, "And books were opened." These books contain the precise, meticulously kept records for every unbeliever. The omniscient God, who sees all and knows all, has been recording in His books every sinful thought, every idle word, and every lawless deed of every unsaved person. Every single sin in the history of the world has been written down in permanent ink by the divine hand. Every selfish deed, every sensual thought, every smutty joke, and every carnal comment has been entered into the heavenly register.

The record will show sins of omission, what each person should have done but failed to do. It will show sins of commission, as all that people should not have done but did do is recorded. Every wrong influence that they exerted upon others as a teenager, every sinful deed that was done in college, every sinful thing that was done in the military, even sins long since forgotten, will be brought out into the open and presented on this last day in court. Skeletons will come dancing out of closets. Secret sins will be shouted from the rooftops on this day.

The book of Ecclesiastes speaks of God's final judgment: "Know that for all these things God will bring you into judgment" (Eccl. 11:9). Solomon concludes with the statement, "For God will bring every deed into judgment, with every secret thing, whether good or evil" (Eccl. 12:14). Jesus reinforces this truth when He says, "I tell you, on the day of judgment people will give account for every careless word they speak" (Matt. 12:36). Again, Jesus warned, "For nothing is hidden that will not be made manifest, nor is anything secret that will not be known and come to light" (Luke 8:17). Jesus is not an idle talker. All that He says is true, and He has stated in no uncertain terms that He will bring every act to judgment.

The author of Hebrews warns, "And no creature is hidden from his sight, but all are naked and exposed to the eyes of him to whom we must give account" (Heb. 4:13). On the last day, as the Lord Jesus Christ is seated upon His throne of judgment, and every lost sinner will stand before Him. Jesus Christ will open the books, and every life will be measured against the holiness of God. In that last day, God will not grade on a curve but will weigh every individual against the absolute, infinite, moral perfection of God Himself. All those outside of Christ will fall woefully short of the glory of God.

Justice Demands Punishment

This verdict leads to dire consequences, as divine justice demands divine punishment for every breach of the divine law. The Bible plainly states, "The soul who sins shall die" (Ezek. 18:4). This truth is repeated throughout the New Testament as well: "For the wages of sin is death" (Rom. 6:23), and "Do not be deceived:

God is not mocked, for whatever one sows, that will he also reap" (Gal. 6:7). The divine sentence is eternal death.

Every sin in the history of the world will be judged by Jesus Christ. No sin will be overlooked by Him on the final day. From the first sin of Adam to the last sin at the end of time, every single offense will be subjected to God's perfect judgment. Every transgression will be punished in Christ at the cross or it will be punished by Christ in hell, but every sin will receive a just recompense.

Think of what it would be like to stand before Jesus Christ in that last day without any forgiveness from God. In that final hour, it will be too late to make things right. There will be no second chance after death. This will be your day to stand in the judgment, and there will be no appeal to a higher court, no reversal of the divine verdict. Every sin you have ever committed in your life will be presented by Christ. You see this whole record, a mountain of sin. You will shrink back and say, "Oh, my God, no." Jesus Christ will say, "This was your life. This is the reality of the sin of your life before you." Jesus Christ, who knows all, sees all, and remembers all, will present His case on that day against every lost sinner. His judgments will be true, and His sentences will come to pass.

Opening the Book of Life

After looking at the books containing each one's deeds, Jesus Christ will open another book, "the book of life" (Rev. 20:12). In this sacred tome are recorded the names of every genuine believer in Jesus Christ. Here is the divine register containing the names of all the elect of God. A sovereign God chose His elect long ago in eternity past and gave them to His Son, the Lord Jesus Christ. Before the foundation of the world, their individual names were written in this book. New names are not being added.

After the Book of Life is opened, Jesus Christ will present His case and unbelievers will find that their names are not written in it. Throughout their life, they never cast themselves upon the mercy of Christ in repentance and faith. Instead, they chose to go their own way and do their own thing. They will see in this last day that they have no right to enter heaven. They will have no claim upon the mercy and forgiveness of God, for they never entrusted their life to Him.

Divine Judgment Executed

Now we read, "And the dead were judged by what was written in the books, according to what they had done" (Rev. 20:12). Understand this—salvation is by grace, and judgment is by works. Each sinner will be strictly judged by the Lord Jesus Christ according to what he did. Inflexible justice will be executed. There will not be one drop of mercy on that day. None will walk away from this scene forgiven. None will be given a second chance. All will be judged according to their deeds. All will be held accountable to the amount of truth they had received. Those who had a greater exposure to the truth of God will be held to an even stricter judgment.

Jesus taught, "Truly, I say to you, it will be more bearable on the day of judgment for the land of Sodom and Gomorrah than for that town" (Matt. 10:15). Sodom and Gomorrah had the most wicked culture on the earth. Yet for those to whom Jesus preached the gospel and who saw Him perform miracles and yet rejected Him, the judgment will be far worse than what awaits the foul people of Sodom and Gomorrah. In this final day, those who had a greater exposure to the truth will have a greater judgment rendered to them, much more severe than for those who had not heard the truth.

The Apostle Paul anticipated this day: "But because of your hard and impenitent heart you are storing up wrath for yourself on the day of wrath when God's righteous judgment will be revealed. He will render to each one according to his works" (Rom. 2:5–6). "For all who have sinned without the law will also perish without the law, and all who have sinned under the law will be judged by the law" (Rom. 2:12). "On that day when, according to my gospel, God judges the secrets of men by Christ Jesus" (Rom. 2:16).

Rendering the Final Verdict

Finally, having examined the evidence and documented the guilt of every lost sinner, the guilty defendants now await the final verdict of this sovereign Judge: "Then Death and Hades were thrown into the lake of fire. . . . And if anyone's name was not found written in the book of life, he was thrown into the lake of fire" (Rev. 20:14–15). There can be no more terrifying description of hell than this—"the lake of fire." In the Bible, the primary picture of hell is fire. This is a frightening image of the eternal abode of fiery torment below. In hell, there exists a "fury of fire that will consume the adversaries" (Heb. 10:27), where "they will be tormented day and night forever and ever" (Rev. 20:10).

Christ Himself, who is omnipresent, will be in hell to personally inflict wrath upon unbelievers. Damned souls "will be tormented with fire and sulfur in the presence of the holy angels and in the presence of the Lamb" (Rev. 14:10). "In the presence of the Lamb" means "before his face" or "face-to-face." The unbelievers will not be separated from Christ but will actually be the object of His direct wrath. Jesus Christ, the righteous judge, will be the executor of His vengeance in hell.

Revelation 20:15 brings this terrifying scene to completion, "If anyone's name was not found written in the book of life, he was thrown into the lake of fire." This day is looming on the horizon and fixed on God's calendar. This fiery hell lasts forever, and it will never come to an end. Throughout all of the ages to come, those who are cast down into this bottomless pit and lake of fire and brimstone that burns forever will never know a moment of relief. There will never be any escape from the infliction of eternal punishment. Rather, throughout all of the ages to come, these damned souls will be the object of God's fury, vengeance, wrath, and judgment.

What Is Your Response?

What should this scene from the last day say to us, who are believers in Jesus Christ? What should this final judgment require of believers? There are two main points of application that we must put into action. Both are critically important as we live with a proper response to this truth.

First, we must be *humbled* by this truth. There but for the grace of God, we would suffer the same torment. There but for the grace of God, we would be judged and condemned. There but for the grace of God, we would be damned forever. The only difference between us and those who will be condemned at the great white throne judgment is the unconditional love and unmerited favor of the Lord Jesus Christ. Every one of us who believes in Jesus Christ deserves to be condemned at this great white throne judgment. We likewise should be cast down into the lake of fire, for we have all sinned and fallen short of the glory of God. Yet, God has taken our many sins and placed them behind His back. Jesus has removed our iniquities from us as far as the east is from the west. Christ has washed away our sins, imputed His perfect righteousness to us, and covered us with His blood, so that our sins will never be brought into account before God.

Let us, therefore, walk in lowly humility before our God. In light of this final day, there is no room for boasting by anyone. What lowliness of mind should grip each one who entrusts himself to Jesus Christ. We have no merit of our own but the merit of Him who lived in perfect obedience to the law and who died for those who have broken this law.

How humbly we should walk before our God. What thanksgiving we should offer to the Lord. There is no condemnation for those who are in Christ Jesus, and nothing will ever separate us from the love of God (Rom. 8:1, 39). How this should cause us to treasure our eternal salvation in Christ. Consider the great sin that has been forgiven you, and consider the great sacrifice that has been offered to take away your sin. Every one of us should walk lowly before our God in great humility.

Second, we must bear *witness* of this truth. The retribution of truth in the final judgment should stir us to evangelism. There are people all around us who have yet to come to Christ, who are outside of the kingdom of God and thus under His wrath. The experience of God's redeeming love is restricted exclusively for those who are inside the Lord Jesus Christ. Those who are outside of Christ are in a fearful place. It is incumbent upon each and every one of us to go into the world and entreat the unconverted to come to the salvation that has already been prepared by Christ.

What responsibility we have to go to our families, friends, classmates, and colleagues with a sense of urgency to share the love of God in the cross of the Lord Jesus Christ. How shall they escape if they neglect so great a salvation? How compulsory it is for us to go into all the world and to preach repentance before God and faith in Jesus Christ. How we must be used by God to reach others so that they may embrace the reality of truth in the word of the cross, rather than one day having to face the final retribution of truth in the final judgment.

SCRIPTURE INDEX

ABOUT THE AUTHOR

Dr. Steven J. Lawson is founder and president of OnePassion Ministries, a ministry that exists to ignite a supreme passion for God and His glory in all people throughout the world, and former senior pastor of Christ Fellowship Baptist Church in Mobile, Ala. He served as a pastor for thirty-four years, having previously served in Arkansas and Alabama. He is a graduate of Texas Tech University (B.B.A.), Dallas Theological Seminary (Th.M.), and Reformed Theological Seminary (D.Min.).

Dr. Lawson is the author of nearly two dozen books, his most recent being *John Knox: Fearless Faith* and *In It to Win It: Pursuing Victory in the One Race That Really Counts*. His other books include *The Daring Mission of William Tyndale*; *Foundations of Grace* and *Pillars of Grace* from the Long Line of Godly Men series; *Famine in the Land: A Passionate Call to Expository Preaching*; *Psalms* volumes 1 and 2 and *Job* in the Holman Old Testament Commentary Series; *Made in Our Image*; and *Absolutely Sure*. His books have been translated into various languages, including Russian, Italian, Portuguese, Spanish, German, Albanian, and Indonesian. He has contributed articles to *Bibliotheca Sacra, The Southern Baptist Journal of Theology, Faith and Mission, Decision* magazine, *Discipleship Journal*, and *Tabletalk*, among other journals and magazines.

Dr. Lawson's pulpit ministry takes him around the world, including Russia, Ukraine, Wales, England, Germany, Italy, Switzerland, New Zealand, Japan, and to many conferences in the United States, including The Shepherd's Conference and Resolved at Grace Community Church in Sun Valley, Calif.

He is professor-in-residence at Truth Remains, a teaching fellow and board member for Ligonier Ministries, and an executive board member for The Master's Seminary and College. He teaches expository preaching in the doctor of ministry program at The Master's Seminary and hosts The Expositors' Conference at Christ Fellowship Baptist Church. Dr. Lawson has participated in the Distinguished Scholars Lecture Series at The Master's Seminary and serves on the advisory council for Samara Preachers' Institute and Theological Seminary in Samara, Russia.

Dr. Lawson and his wife, Anne, have three sons, Andrew, James, and John, and a daughter, Grace Anne.